IRRESISTIBLE REVOLUTION

Marxism's Goal Of Conquest &
The Unmaking Of The American Military

IRRESISTIBLE REVOLUTION

Marxism's Goal Of Conquest &
The Unmaking Of The American Military

MATTHEW
LOHMEIER

First Edition: May 2021

Cover design by David Christenson
Internal design by Kevin Merrell

ISBN: 978-1-7370673-2-0 (paperback)
ISBN: 978-1-7370673-0-6 (hardcover)

The conclusions and opinions expressed in this book are those of the author. They do not necessarily reflect the official position of the United States Government, Department of Defense, or United States Space Force.

www.matthewlohmeier.com

To my wonderful parents

And for my wife and children

TABLE OF CONTENTS

Introduction **1**

PART I: THE GREATNESS OF THE AMERICAN IDEAL

CHAPTER 1 / Transforming American History **8**

CHAPTER 2 / America's Founding Philosophy **26**

PART II: MARXISM'S GOAL OF CONQUEST

CHAPTER 3 / Marx, Marxism, And Revolution, Part 1 **46**

CHAPTER 4 / Marx, Marxism, And Revolution, Part 2 **66**

CHAPTER 5 / Marxism's Many Faces **84**

PART III: UNMAKING AMERICA'S MILITARY

CHAPTER 6 / The New American Military Culture **124**

CHAPTER 7 / The Wrath To Come **162**

Afterword **190**

Suggested Reading **192**

Acknowledgments **196**

Endnotes **197**

About the Author **216**

DISCLAIMER

The conclusions and opinions expressed in this book are those of the author. They do not necessarily reflect the official position of the United States Government, Department of Defense, or United States Space Force.

THESE ARE THE TIMES *that try men's souls. The summer soldier and the sunshine patriot will, in this crisis, shrink from the service of their country; but he that stands by it now, deserves the love and thanks of man and woman. Tyranny, like hell, is not easily conquered; yet we have this consolation with us, that the harder the conflict, the more glorious the triumph. What we obtain too cheap, we esteem too lightly: it is dearness only that gives every thing its value. Heaven knows how to put a proper price upon its goods; and it would be strange indeed if so celestial an article as freedom should not be highly rated.*

Thomas Paine
December 23, 1776

INTRODUCTION

TO APPRECIATE JUST HOW DISPROPORTIONATE, ugly, or evil a thing is, sometimes one must first comprehend what is balanced, beautiful, and good. To recognize approaching danger or impending chaos is often to have first been properly oriented to safety and order. Thus, opposites serve an important educational purpose—provide a necessary contrast—both enabling and requiring human discernment as well as constructing a context for the exercise of free will.

I recently attended a weekend series of lectures on geometry that drove home these ideas to me. The simple use of a straightedge and compass allows the geometer to construct basic geometric shapes that become building blocks for the construction of other common and even more complex shapes and symbols. From circles, triangles, and squares, for example, I constructed perfect pentagons and hexagons. Using those same basic building blocks of the circle, triangle, and square, I constructed various root rectangles and measured the proportion of the golden section (the ratio of 1 to 1.618033989...), which was used in the monumental architecture of Egypt and elsewhere in the ancient world. My brief exposure bestowed a heightened perception of the beauty and symmetry throughout nature and improved my discernment of disunity and the disproportionate. It was like I had acquired better eyes by which those things that were before unrecognizable to me became apparent.

This book is largely about Marxism, something that is ugly and which can even be appropriately associated with evil aims and ends.[1] But it is unlikely the reader will fully appreciate or see its ugliness for what it is unless this book begins with an examination of something that is beautiful and right—something Marxism seeks to dismantle, disrupt, and destroy. The three-part framework of this book has been constructed with that in mind. It begins with a discussion of the greatness of the American ideal, transitions to an examination of the history and overarching narrative of Marxist ideology, and concludes by looking into the ongoing transformation of America's military culture, while also providing a warning about where this country is headed if we choose to not make an immediate course correction.

Marxism has begun its destructive conquest of even the United States military, its most alarming manifestation in the United States to date. This reality will likely come as a surprise to many Americans, including our military servicemembers.

This book, however, is not so narrowly focused as to only discuss the appearance of Marxist ideology within the uniformed services. Becoming aware of the Marxist conquest of American society, one will never again look at things in the same way. Mainstream media, social media, the public education system, including the university, as well as federal agencies have all become vessels of various schools of thought that are rooted in Marxist ideology—an ideology bent on the destruction of America's history and founding philosophy, of Western tradition, specifically Judeo-Christian values, and of patriotism and conservatism. The problem has become systemic, a tragedy considering that the defeat of Marxist-communist ideology was the very cause against which our nation spent great treasures of blood and iron during much of the twentieth century.

At the very same time that we see the proliferation of Marxist ideology, there have arisen multifarious accusations of other forms of systemic injustice, such as racism, that are wrecking civil society.

This is not a coincidence.

The many critical and antagonistic narratives about America all serve one primary purpose—dividing the American people. Therefore, the audience for this book is much broader than just US military servicemembers—it is hoped that this book proves instructive to every American citizen. If we continue to suffer it, Marxism's dreadful march will not stop short of the overthrow of the current social and political order.

What I address in this book is directly relevant to an ongoing conversation about "extremism within the ranks" of our uniformed services that, by now, most readers have certainly heard about in the news. Marxism and Marxist organizations constitute a form of extremism, at least from the American perspective and as defined in Department of Defense Instruction (DoDI) 1325.06, *Handling Dissident and Protest Activities Among Members of the Armed Forces.* In that short, ten-page Instruction, military personnel are prohibited from advocating or participating in extremist "doctrine, ideology, or causes," such as those that "advance, encourage, or advocate illegal discrimination based on race, creed, color, sex, religion, ethnicity, or national origin or those that advance, encourage, or advocate the use of force, violence, or criminal activity or otherwise advance efforts to deprive individuals of their civil rights."[2] The same Instruction goes on to state that military personnel "must reject" active participation in such ideologies and causes.

A recent memorandum from the Secretary of Defense dated February 5, 2021, was distributed across the services to "commanding officers and supervisors at all levels," directing a stand-down to address extremism within the ranks. In it, Secretary Lloyd Austin referenced the above DoDI, and concluded his memorandum with the following injunction to all servicemembers:

This stand-down is just the first initiative of what I believe *must be a concerted effort to better educate ourselves and our people about the scope of this problem* and to develop sustainable ways to eliminate the corrosive effects that extremist ideology and conduct have on the workforce. *We owe it to the oath we each took and the trust the American people have in our institution.*"[3] (Italics added)

Additionally, in a 70-page *Extremism Stand-down Day Playbook* distributed to commanders and supervisors by the Air Force, servicemembers were instructed to "stand up for each other." "Everyone has a responsibility to say something when they see impermissible behavior," the training playbook explains, and to "stand against" ideologies and causes that are detrimental to good order and discipline.

Despite the fact that Marxism hardly requires a new expositor, perhaps my contribution will nevertheless prove unique. Some will say I am out of my lane as an active-duty servicemember writing about something that is political in nature. But I disagree. Given the context of our day, which I describe in this book, and the invitation of the Secretary of Defense noted above, this work presently becomes relevant to our ongoing education and dialogue. To that end, this book is part memoir and part academic, written through the lens of an active-duty servicemember, though I, of course, cannot and do not presume to speak on behalf of the United States Defense Department or the Space Force.

This book is my best effort to participate in that "concerted effort to better educate ourselves and our people about the scope" of the problem of dangerous ideologies that threaten to undermine our Nation, our Constitution, and our way of life, and to "stand up for" our young servicemembers whom I lead and serve. I add my voice to that of Secretary Austin's that "we owe it to the oath we each took" and to the American people to do so. If the American military ever has a hope of returning to being a nonpartisan institution, then it is critical that someone publicly identify the subversive and ideological agenda that is underway.

While it is my hope that the American people might better understand and appreciate what follows, the military servicemember in particular is at the forefront of my intentions. It is sad, but true, that many young servicemembers who take the oath to defend the Constitution do not fully appreciate liberty, the civil society, republicanism, and economic prosperity; but what is worse is that they do not fear their loss. Without becoming rooted in a proper understanding of the greatness of the American ideal, these great young Americans may never appreciate their liberty or recognize when it is under attack.

Today's military professional shoulders a difficult burden. In a world in which postmodernist, politically correct, neo-Marxist activists have politicized every aspect of human existence, the young military professional is reminded still that he or she must remain apolitical. What this amounts to in practice strips these men and women of their rights to share their views or beliefs openly on just about any subject—unless of course they, too, share what has become the progressive Leftist paradigm.

Though I have done my best in this book to provide useful information, I have undoubtedly omitted relevant content that would further substantiate my work. Such is the nature of any book dealing with current events as they unfold. With every passing week, I encounter new information in the form of news articles and emails that I wish I had time to work into the text. But because to spend additional time on the work is to endlessly encounter the same problem, and because my effectiveness is relegated only to what spare time I can find before and after the duty hours of my full-time job as a commander, it seems prudent to me to publish the work now and to present what I hope will be useful to many people despite its current deficiencies, whatever they might be.

PART I

THE GREATNESS OF THE AMERICAN IDEAL

TO WHOM SHALL I SPEAK *and give warning, that they may hear?*

Thus says the Lord: Stand in the ways and see, and ask for the old paths where is the good way, and walk therein, and you shall find rest for your souls. But they said, We will not walk therein. Also, I set watchmen over you, saying, Listen to the sound of the trumpet. But they said, We will not listen.

Jeremiah

CHAPTER 1

TRANSFORMING AMERICAN HISTORY

We are approaching a major turning point in world history,
in the history of civilization. ...It is a juncture at which settled
concepts suddenly become hazy, lose their precise contours,
at which our familiar and commonly used words lose their
meaning, become empty shells, and methods which have been
reliable for many centuries no longer work.

Alexander Solzhenitsyn, July 9, 1975

BECAUSE OF THE WISDOM *and encouragement of good parents, I decided*
to attend the United States Air Force Academy following high school. I
got in because I was good at basketball, not because I had ever been a
serious student. Life at the Academy was difficult but rewarding. The first
two years were particularly taxing, especially for those like me who had
just left home for the first time in their lives. When my incoming class of
freshmen and I first arrived, we had everything stripped from us—civilian
clothes, cars, cell phones, other personal belongings, and even our hair.

Thus began my initiation into a respectable tradition, one for which
I have been profoundly grateful. That tradition taught us not to lie, steal,
or cheat, nor tolerate among us anyone who does. It was a tradition of
patriotism. The Academy was a place where I learned that no honor
was granted short of hard work and merit. There, I learned personal
responsibility and accountability. By the time I had graduated, I had

ironed more shirts, polished more shoes, and made more beds than I care to remember.

Perhaps among the greatest aspects of my education, though, is that I was taught firsthand what it feels like to have one's rights taken from them, and to appreciate just how tangible those rights really are. Yet, despite being stripped of an autonomy of action that one might rightly call liberty, I could nevertheless sense what it meant to retain a sacred autonomy over one's own thoughts—the freedom to think and believe what I wanted. That freedom, one's free will, no man could take.

There were other memorable experiences I had while at the Academy. One in particular is worth noting. During my junior year, I was selected to travel to China as part of a small US delegation of cadets. Over spring break, we traveled to the People's Liberation Army Air Force (PLAAF) Academy in Chang Chun, China, north of North Korea. It was March, and I remember it being very cold during the week we were there. While there, I was sponsored by and slept in a shared room with two other Chinese cadets. Since I spoke Mandarin it was easy for me to enjoy dialogue with them during our brief stay.

I remember the cold cement floors in their cadet dormitories. I remember the small buckets of water sitting outside their bedrooms lining the hallway—these they used to briefly wash up and brush their teeth before retiring for the night. Our delegation was not aware of showers in the dorms, at least we did not see or have access to them while there.

I remember these two cadets with whom I stayed—underclassmen, though I do not remember what year they were—sitting up in bed in the shape of an "L," with their legs tucked under uncomfortably tight sheets, their hands gripping the tops of those sheets on either side of their bodies, looking straight forward, and waiting for upperclassmen to blow whistles in the hall signaling that it was time to sleep. The whistles blew and, on cue, these cadets lay back in their beds and ceased all discussion. It was really quite a sight.

What I remember most, however, was the brief conversation I had with these two in the private confines of their own room before it was time for bed. I do not remember most of what was said, or for how long we talked. *As you might imagine, they were interested in me and I in them. They appeared to take a liking to me, and I remember liking them. We did not waste much of our time engaged in small talk, but instead tried to learn as much as we might about each other in the little time we had together. Even though before our visit our small US delegation had been warned which things we were not allowed to talk about, we college students had enough curiosity toward one another that these social guidelines seemed fungible. Eventually, beliefs were discussed, albeit briefly.*

"What are your beliefs," I asked. I assumed I would learn that they were Buddhist or Taoist.

"We believe in Marxism," came the reply.

"Is that how you were raised?"

"No."

"Do your parents believe in Marxism?" At this, they seemed hesitant to answer. Looking back now, I cannot help but wonder if we were being recorded.

"No. My parents are Buddhist," one of them answered.

At the time, I really had no clue what that meant—to "believe in Marxism"—and I did not have the interest to study it until many years later. These young cadets went on to assure me that all PLAAF *servicemembers believed in Marxism.*

I could not help but sense the humanity hiding behind the rigid façade worn by these two young PLAAF *cadets. They were just like me in a way. They, too, had left their homes and were serving their country. I am sure they, too, sometimes longed for home. One might presume they were just as free as I was, at least in the way I mentioned earlier—in the way that is internal to and inherent in all humans, namely, the freedom to think and believe what they wanted. And yet, that sacred space, too, had somehow been subjugated and tread upon by the regime in which they lived. The military tradition into which they were initiates was, in fact, quite different than mine. I perceived that these young people sought to retain their humanity despite their context, but that somehow, to use Solzhenitsyn's phrase, "breathing and consciousness" had been taken from them. I felt compassion for them.*

I was grateful to get back to America and, for one of the first times since beginning my education there years earlier, to the Air Force Academy. The best way I might describe the feeling I had when I walked off the airplane and set foot back in America was that it was like a breath of fresh air—call it freedom, perhaps. It was that same tangible feeling I had come to recognize when once my rights had been stripped from me as a young freshman. America was great.

Resurrecting the Ministry of Truth

THERE IS A STRUGGLE OVER the meaning of America presently underway that is at the heart of a social and political polarization that threatens to permanently fracture American civil society. That struggle is fueled by radical revisions of American history that are more ideological than historical, and by the proliferation of false narratives intent on breeding contempt for America's heritage and national identity.

In his classic and never-more-relevant dystopian novel *Nineteen Eighty-Four*, George Orwell describes the bizarre totalitarian society in which Winston Smith, the book's main character, lives and works. There, in that fictionalized future, "Big Brother" is always watching and listening, the "Thought Police" are always on the move in search of "Thoughtcrimes," and government employees are constantly, daily, subjected to training sessions and meetings referred to as the "Two Minutes Hate." Those in society who dare maintain traditional views, views contrary to the party line—who are perhaps, as Orwell describes, the sole guardians "of truth and sanity in a world of lies"—are derided as heretics by "The Party." The people are trained to hate these heretics and target them. Suspects are watched day and night for any signs of unorthodoxy. They are eventually rounded up and arrested. "People simply disappeared....Your name was removed from the registers, every record of everything you had ever done was wiped out, your one-time existence was denied and then forgotten. You were abolished, annihilated."[4]

Where Winston works, in the Records Department of *The Ministry of Truth*, employees are busy working on the "news, entertainment, education, and the fine arts." They write the history, the news, and the education curriculum. But it is the Party that determines and defines reality—whether to create, revise, or destroy history, how to re-define words, which thoughts are criminal and which are allowed, all are decisions that are made above the employees' paygrade. Their job is simply to impose the manufactured reality. And if society accepts the lie the Party imposes—if all records tell the same tale—then the lie "passed into history and became the truth."

The Ministry of Truth, deliberately representative of Stalin's Communist propaganda mill, employed a simple and effective strategy: "Who controls the past controls the future: who controls the present controls the past."[5] It was this kind of manipulative control in the former Soviet Union that led to the dissident joke: "In the Soviet Union the future is known; it's the past that is always changing." Thus, all that is needed to assert control is an unending series of victories over people's memory.

Russian mathematician and anti-Soviet dissident Igor Shafarevich explained that the Soviet Communist regime was always rewriting history "so as to belittle the people's national identity" and destroy the "national culture."[6] In his essay "Separation or Reconciliation?—The Nationalities Question in the USSR," Shafaravich writes of the Soviet's methods: "Historical relics are destroyed instead of preserved, ancient cities and streets are given new names." It seemed to him and other Russians as if every action taken by the state was meant to "stamp out any manifestation of Russian national consciousness."[7]

We are witnessing the resurrection of Orwell's Ministry of Truth in our own day, in our very own country.

Newspapers across the country are establishing initiatives to revise old news articles that reflect unfavorably on "public figures" and "disproportionately impact people of color." The *Boston Globe*, for example, announced that its "Fresh Start" initiative allows people to request past stories be updated or anonymized, eliminating stains that may prove embarrassing if left in the record.[8] The committee of ten that is responsible for adjudicating requests for historical patchwork concede that removing certain stories in their entirety from Google searches may be the best approach in some cases. There will no doubt be a learning curve for these American Winstons—after all, at the moment it is merely "an experiment," says the *Globe*.[9]

As described, these initiatives seem well-intentioned enough and limited in scope. But there have recently been far-more dangerous efforts underway to re-write American history and thus control the future. The *New York Times'* "1619 Project" is one such effort.

The 1619 Project was published in a special issue of *The New York Times Magazine* in August 2019 on the 400th anniversary of English pirates landing at least twenty African slaves on American soil. The 100-page magazine project is an attempt to "reframe American history," according to Jake Silverstein, the *Times'* editor in chief, and proudly "decenter whiteness," according to Nikole Hannah-Jones, the project's creator and lead essayist.[10]

And reframe history it does. Hannah-Jones' lead essay asserts that 1619 is the year that marks America's founding—not 1776, as we have always been taught—and that the real reason for the American Revolution was to preserve the institution of slavery—an astounding claim that cannot be substantiated from contemporary historical evidence, which is why Hannah-Jones does not include citations in her essay. In the same essay, Hannah-Jones claims that the US Constitution is a "decidedly undemocratic document," that "anti-black racism runs in the very DNA of this country," and that America's "founding ideals were false when they were written."[11]

She further asserts that the American practice of slavery "within the 13 colonies" at the time of its traditionally dated founding, was "unlike anything that had existed in the world before."[12] Besides being un-American and untrue, these views put Hannah-Jones at odds with former slave Frederick Douglass—the most prominent abolitionist in US history—who referred to the Constitution as a "glorious liberty document," and also with Martin Luther King, Jr., who referred to the Declaration and Constitution as "those great wells of democracy," which the founding fathers "dug deep."[13] To accept her view is to reject theirs. Of the many references to the Declaration of Independence and Constitution made throughout the project's essays, none are positive or complimentary; they are referred to only with criticism and contempt.

As an active-duty servicemember who swears an oath to defend the Constitution, it should be readily clear why I find the 1619 Project repulsive. As an American who loves my country and has studied its history, Hannah-Jones' work is unimpressive. For those who have developed a sense for the look and feel of anti-American propaganda, you recognize it almost immediately in this special project of the *Times*.

But beyond Hannah-Jones, you may wonder, what do the project's other essayists write?

Throughout the essays runs the theme of a capitalist ruling class being ever-pitted against a victimized working class—Marx's old bourgeoisie versus proletariat narrative, which will be discussed in greater detail in Chapters 3 and 4. The project's essays further claim that racism is an unchangeable aspect of American society—that "our founding fathers may not have actually believed in the ideals they espoused, but black people did."[14] Blacks continue to face "rampant discrimination" in America.[15] It is asserted that "extremism…has taken over the Republican party," and that nineteenth-century slaveholders had a prominent influence on "modern right-wing thinking."[16] Slavery, the essayists assert, is the reason American capitalism is so brutal.[17] Slavery is the reason why whites are addicted to sugar.[18] And slavery is even the reason there are rush-hour traffic jams in modern cities.[19] Slavery, therefore, is not just an important element of American history; according to the essayists of the 1619 Project, it is the centerpiece.

Race and identity-based politics become the prominent dividing line between Americans when the American story is left in the slippery hands of these employees at the *Times'* Ministry of Truth. As some of America's most prominent academic historians from across the political spectrum have asserted: this is not history, it is ideology.[20] It is false.

Slavery, without question, was an ugly and brutally dehumanizing institution—an important and inescapable part of the American story. Americans understand this whether or not they accept the historical narrative framed by the writers at the *Times*. During the nineteenth century, the South particularly became ever more committed to slave labor, in what turned into a self-reinforcing cycle.[21] As prominent historian Wilfred McClay observes, "the South would become fatally committed to a brutal social and economic system that was designed for the lucrative production of cotton on a massive scale but that achieved such productivity at an incalculable cost in human and moral terms."[22] Indeed, Americans today believe slavery to be wretched—as have many Americans throughout our country's history. And for the Old South, slavery placed the region on a collision course with fundamental American ideals that ended in what was undoubtedly the country's most destructive war.

We also understand that the institution of slavery was not an American invention. It was not even a European invention. Slavery has existed in human societies for thousands of years. As author and president of the National Association of Scholars Peter W. Wood points out, slave capture and trading were pursued on an enormous scale by the Arabs in north and east Africa.[23] And when Europeans arrived on the Atlantic coast of Africa in the fifteenth century, they discovered that slavery was a deeply embedded practice in the native kingdoms there. Wood further explains: "By comparison with the

Caribbean and South American colonies, the English colonies that would one day become the United States were lightly touched by the slave trade, especially during their first hundred years."²⁴ The 1619 Project argues to the contrary that slavery was fundamental to the formation of American social order and culture. This is an overdrawn and exaggerated picture that is deliberately crafted to blind readers to America's founding philosophy and the greatness of the American ideal. It is intended to be divisive.

Despite the facts, on May 4, 2020, Hannah-Jones was awarded the once-prestigious Pulitzer Prize for her work. Normally, the Pulitzer is not awarded to individuals whose material is considered *not* credible by a majority of experts in the field. When the editors responsible for the 1619 Project have been confronted with errors and contradictions of their portrayal of American history, rather than intelligently articulate an historically informed position, they have retreated into the postmodern claim that it is *all a matter of interpretation*.²⁵ Indeed, so it is. But not all interpretations are of equal value. Criticisms of the work have predictably been labeled "racist," and Hannah-Jones has disdained her critics as "old, white male historians."²⁶

Without her audacious claims, it is unlikely Hannah-Jones would have received the Pulitzer, and the project the attention it has. And while her race-based fantasy has garnered the attention of many critics, it has also secured the support of other groups who share her radical political agenda—groups such as the National Education Association (NEA), the nation's largest teacher's union, and a Marxist group called Black Lives Matter at School, among others.

In 2020, the NEA worked with the *Times* to distribute copies of the 1619 Project to educators and activists around the country to help them develop a deeper "understanding of systemic racism." A "1619 Project Booklet" has since seen broad distribution in connection with the efforts of the Black Lives Matter at School group. The "Booklet" itself is a publication of the Zinn Education Project, named for the late Howard Zinn, a radical Marxist historian. The

Zinn Education Project has been active in offering to distribute and teach the 1619 Project material to educators across the country. Not coincidentally, Zinn's own narrative of American history first published in the 80s, *A People's History of the United States*, the work for which he is best known, shares the same critical and cynical character as the 2019 *Times* project. In Zinn's work, he goes as far as to admit his "hope" that there will be a people's revolution in the United States.[27] One of the strategies that must be pursued in order to secure that end is the dismantling of traditional history and its replacement with a revised history that works on the "imagination" of the people.[28] For "history which keeps alive the memory of people's resistance suggests new definitions of power."[29]

If you are not already making the connection between the aims of these efforts, let me try to help you with a question. Why is it, do you think, that Marxist education organizations are interested in getting the 1619 Project into the hands of as many Americans as possible? If the answer to that question eludes you, it will be clear soon enough.

The problem is not merely that Hannah-Jones' 1619 Project is bad history—there is plenty of bad history floating around. No—her ideologically guided, racially divisive history has become a dangerous weapon in the hands of those who hate America and would like to see it dismantled, fundamentally transformed, or destroyed.

Hannah-Jones, who received a fellowship to travel to Cuba to study its Communist universal healthcare and education systems before she made her attempt to reframe American history, has no problem putting her strong disliking for America on public display. And she has taken heat for her views. Ironically, even Socialists from the world Trotskyist movement were so off-put by Hannah-Jones' remarks made during a speech she delivered at New York University in 2019 that they took to the web criticizing her, saying: "there was not a single statement made by Hannah-Jones that evening, on historical issues, that withstands serious examination."[30] They condemned her remarks about the Holocaust, and attacked her comparisons of the United States with Nazi Germany, saying that she "came dangerously close to endorsing the conception that genocide...was a solution to inherent racism."[31]

These hateful views are not a recent development, however. Years earlier, in a letter to the editor of Notre Dame's *Observer* that a younger Hannah-Jones would never have anticipated would be paraded for the world to see, she wrote that "the white race is the biggest murderer, rapist, pillager, and thief of the modern world....whites have always been an unjust, jealous, unmerciful, avaricious, and blood-thirsty set of beings." In the same letter she also wrote that Christopher Columbus is "no different then [sic] Hitler," and insisted that white European descendants of America's settlers continue to be "bloodsuckers in our communities."[32]

The 1619 mythology created by this angry writer is now being packaged up and used in public schools and university classrooms across America—so far, 4,500 of them at the time of this writing—to serve as the rising generation's first introduction to *real* American history. It will reach millions of Americans who never heard of the original 1619 Project, but who are swept up in its endless reverberations that wash over popular culture.[33] Its effect upon Americans will be the same as that inflicted upon Russians under Communist rule: "generations of Russians [were] brought up on such a horrendous version of Russian history that all they want to do is try and forget [they] ever had a past at all."[34] It is bent on breeding black resentment and white guilt—a dreadful combination. To lose a sense of our history is to lose a sense for what unites us as one people.

Beyond Partisan Politics

Among the reasons I have taken interest in the 1619 Project is that it has already begun reshaping the American military culture, and with disastrous effect. As shall be seen in this book, the military's "Diversity and Inclusion" trainings—as well as other dialogues about race that are foisted upon young people in uniform—are increasingly grounded in the misunderstandings propounded by these *Times* ideologues. Racial identity is becoming a defining characteristic of military forces whose primary identity would otherwise naturally be linked to an oath and a uniform.

Ask yourself these questions:

Do you like the idea of your country's uniformed servicemembers believing the narrative of American history that Communist-Cuba-loving, white-hating Hannah-Jones, Marxist Black Lives Matter at School, and the Marxist Zinn Education Project prescribe?

Is their version of American history true?

Does it appear to you that there is an agenda at play?

Does this ideology unify the country? Is it intended to unify?

If you are a servicemember, have you seen these trainings improve your unit's cohesiveness? Or has it made groups of people increasingly suspicious of one another based on their racial identities?

Every American has to grapple with questions such as these. We have to figure out where we stand. And for active-duty servicemembers, these are not merely partisan political matters about which you are not allowed a public opinion—they are a form of *absolute* politics. As servicemembers, you are left to choose whether you believe in the greatness of the American ideal, or a Marxist delusion.

The President's Advisory 1776 Commission

America was founded on certain core beliefs that the 1619 Project seeks to uproot and replace. Because many if not most Americans have always believed in and sought to live up to those core beliefs, ours is the most successful multi-racial country in world history. None come close. The 1619 Project is actively undoing that, too. The degree to which the United States has succeeded in living up to its founding ideals is reflected in the fact that two million black Africans have legally immigrated to America in the last half-century alone, in addition to the millions of others who have come from across the globe. Why would they do that if America is inherently and irredeemably racist and evil? They would not. Many of these immigrants know what real racism looks like.

To combat the ideologically driven 1619 Project, on November 2, 2020, President Trump established by executive order "the President's Advisory 1776 Commission." The declared purpose of the Commission was to "enable a rising generation to understand the history and principles of the founding of the United States in 1776 and to strive to form a more perfect Union."[35]

The Commission's first responsibility was to produce a report summarizing the principles of America's founding that was "accurate, honest, unifying, inspiring, and ennobling."[36] This was accomplished when on January 18, 2021 the Commission released a 40-page report—fortunately released just two days before the Commission was terminated by executive order on President Joe Biden's first day in office. The Commission's abolition was among President Biden's first orders of business because, as he explained in his inaugural address, we need true history, not "lies—lies told for power and for profit."[37] He also called the Commission's efforts "offensive" and "counterfactual."[38]

President Biden was not alone in his criticism of the 1776 Commission's report. The White House and various academics on the Left have spoken out against the report produced by the Commission, saying that Trump published the report "to bend history" as part of a last-ditch political stunt, calling it "right-wing propaganda," and saying that it seeks to "erase America's history of racial injustice."[39] The work's authors have been accused of creating an 11th-hour "hack-job" that "belongs in the trash."[40] Their summary of America's founding principles is labeled "white nationalist" and "radical" in its framing, and the group is reproached as possessing no serious academic credentials.[41] Ibram X. Kendi, an increasingly popular scholar and historian of racism at Boston University, called the report "the last great lie from a Trump administration of great lies."[42] Sam Wineburg, an education professor at Stanford and head of the university's History Education Group, dismissed the Commission's work, saying: "The 1776 document doesn't unify Americans but divides them further."[43]

So, we are left to ask, what was in this report that was so divisive? What in it constitutes the "lies" about which Americans are being warned? What in the report is "offensive," and who wrote these offensive lies? What in it constitutes "white nationalist" garbage?

The Commission's sixteen-person roster was not announced until December 2020. In the few short weeks that followed, the group formally met only twice—once in person in Washington, DC, and once virtually. In anticipation of its impending abolition, the group worked around the clock to produce an accurate summary of America's founding principles that it hoped could be widely shared to combat the ongoing sinister transformation of American history. Despite what online critics claim, the group that accomplished that work is, in fact, comprised of well-respected American academics and historians who have demonstrated decades of serious scholarship and who have a long-proven record of conservatism and patriotism—the only obvious reason for the immediate criticisms leveled at the group by the progressive Left.

Larry P. Arnn, who has served as the twelfth president of the private Hillsdale College for over twenty years, was appointed as chair of the Commission. Arnn is a professor of history and politics, and formerly served as President of the Claremont Institute, an education and research institution based in Southern California. While at Claremont, Arnn was also chairman of the California Civil Rights Initiative (Proposition 209), which, upon approval in November 1996, amended the state constitution prohibiting consideration of race, sex, or ethnicity in state hiring, contracting, and admissions practices. Online professional critics have tried labeling Arnn a racist since the 1776 Report has been released.[44]

Arnn's vice-chair for the Commission is the highly respected, black female academic, Carol Swain, who grew up in poverty but rose to become a professor of law and political science at Vanderbilt University, and whose expertise spans issues of race, immigration, representation, and the US Constitution. Since creation of the Commission, Swain has been labeled a "far-right" activist who is complicit in an attempted "coup" to "overthrow the legitimately elected incoming administration"—an accusation brought against her by an "award-winning reporter" in response to her outrageously seditious tweet amidst the former President's contestation of the November 2020 election results: "Stand strong, Mr. President. We have your back!" Swain tweeted.[45]

Matthew Spalding was appointed to serve as the Commission's executive director. Spalding is a professor of constitutional government and a best-selling author of books about the US Government and Constitution and has also authored biographies of the founders. He was formerly the vice president of American Studies at the Heritage Foundation.

Other Commission members include Jerry Davis, President of the College of the Ozarks and a college president of 44 years; Michael Farris, Chancellor of Patrick Henry College, a private liberal arts non-denominational Christian school, and CEO of an organization called Alliance Defending Freedom; Mike Gonzalez, an author and senior fellow at The Heritage Foundation; Victor Davis Hanson, a famous classicist, military historian, prolific author, senior fellow at the Hoover Institution, and professor emeritus at California State University, Fresno; Charles Kesler, a professor of Government at Claremont McKenna College and author of books about America's founding and founding documents; Peter Kirsanow, a black attorney and the longest-serving member of the United States Commission on Civil Rights; and Thomas Lindsay, a distinguished senior fellow of higher education and constitutional studies at the Texas Public Policy Foundation—a 501(c)3 non-profit, non-partisan research institute—who has also served as a dean, provost, and college president; among others. Additionally, other prominent public figures agreed to serve on the Commission as ex-officio members. Among them are Michael Pompeo, former Secretary of State; Ben Carson, former Secretary of Urban Housing and Development; and Christopher C. Miller, former acting Secretary of Defense.

These impressive individuals are the ones being criticized for their lack of credentials, and who are being labeled "offensive," "radical," "racist," "far right-wing," "white nationalist," and "revisionist." They are the ones, it is alleged, that are causing division in our country—the ones spreading the lies.

As for the work produced by the group in January 2021, there is nothing novel in the Commission's report. Unlike the 1619 Project, it is succinct and easy to understand for all Americans. It is a best-effort attempt at a faithful framework about which the details of American history might be placed and properly interpreted. It does not turn a blind eye to the messes and troubles of America's past, as asserted by its critics, but rather emphasizes how understanding and learning from our past mistakes empowers us to live up to our founding ideals.

The report's authors explain the purposes and meaning of the Declaration of Independence and Constitution, with which we spend more time in the following chapter. They assert that "America's founding principles are true not because any generation...has lived them perfectly, but because they are based upon the eternal truths of the human condition."[46] They continue:

[America's founding principles] are rooted in our capacity for evil and power for good, our longing for truth and striving for justice, our need for order and our love of freedom. Above all else, these principles recognize the worth, equality, potential, dignity, and glory of each and every man, woman, and child created in the image of God.

Throughout our history, our heroes—men and women, young and old, black and white, of many faiths and from all parts of the world—have changed America for the better not by abandoning these truths, but by appealing to them. Upon these universal ideals, they built a great nation, unified a strong people, and formed a beautiful way of life worth defending.

To be an American means something noble and good. It means treasuring freedom and embracing the vitality of self-government....

When we appreciate America for what she truly is, we know that our Declaration is worth preserving, our Constitution worth defending, our fellow citizens worth loving, and our country worth fighting for.[47] (Italics added)

The 1776 Commission's work carries unifying potential for America—the opportunity to rally around a proper understanding of the principles that gave shape to a uniquely American national identity. Take the time to read the report for yourself.[48]

As noted above, these are things deliberately criticized or omitted by Hannah-Jones and the other essayists of the 1619 Project. After all, as Zinn believed, they are relegated to work in the "realm of imagination" to some degree in order to suggest "new definitions of power" to those they hope might join in the revolution.

The nation is rapidly polarizing around the distinct narratives of American history introduced in this chapter. These opposing and incompatible beliefs about America form the basis for divergent value systems—disparate national cultures and identities increasingly alien to and hostile towards one another. This book explores some of the driving forces behind this polarization—specifically, Marxist ideology and Marxism's goal of conquest—and discusses how it is that we have succumbed to it as a country generally and within the military specifically. Before we get there, however, we spend more time with America's founding philosophy.

Despite the 1776 Commission's termination, and though they receive no remuneration for their efforts (undermining any allegations that the group is motivated by "power and profit"), the group's members continue the work of promulgating this more "accurate, honest, unifying, inspiring, and ennobling" version of US history. Their hope in doing so is that, in the words of Lincoln, the truths of America's founding principles, which are "applicable to all men and all times," may prove "a rebuke and a stumbling-block to the very harbingers of re-appearing tyranny and oppression" that we see in our own day.

CHAPTER 2

AMERICA'S FOUNDING PHILOSOPHY

Now, my countrymen, if you have been taught doctrines conflicting with the great landmarks of the Declaration of Independence; if you have listened to the suggestions which would take away from the grandeur, and mutilate the fair symmetry of its proportions; if you have been inclined to believe that all men are not created equal in those inalienable rights enumerated by our chart of liberty, let me entreat you to come back.

Abraham Lincoln

I WAS SURPRISED BY WHAT I ENCOUNTERED last year after taking command of an operational squadron in the Space Force. During my first month in command, military professionals across the base—predominantly Air and Space Force personnel—were asked by base leadership to watch two videos in preparation for a "virtual wingman day," during which trained facilitators would mediate discussions on race and inclusion. This, in the aftermath of the death of George Floyd.

The first video the base was asked to watch portrays American history as fraught with racism from 1619 till the present—"400 years of white supremacy," is how the film's director describes it. The film teaches that the US Constitution codified a racist social order intended to allow whites to remain in power and subjugate and oppress blacks, and that we as a nation have never escaped from that foundation of racism. Further, that upon ratification of the Constitution, "white supremacy was now the official policy of the United States of America." At one point, reference is made to former Senate Majority Leader Mitch McConnell, and it is asserted that because the mentality of white supremacy has become engrained in our nation's psyche, he, and other whites like him, do not want blacks "to get too far." The idea is that the racism of these white people is true whether they recognize it or not. They simply cannot help it.

The second video portrays Republican politicians as racist, claiming, for example, that George Bush won his election by causing Americans to fear black people, and also showing clips of Donald Trump before the 2016 election that cast him in a negative light, insinuating that he has fueled systemic racism in America. Later in the video, President Trump (who was President and commander in chief both at the time the video was created as well as when it was distributed to the base) is cast in a terrible light—and out of context—directly implying that he enjoys oppressing blacks and keeping minorities in an inferior status. Democrat politicians, on the other hand, are portrayed as aiding the black community. There are favorable clips of Barack Obama, and Bill and Hillary Clinton, who all had, at least as depicted in the video, undoubtedly contributed greatly to the eradication of anti-black racism and the systemic oppression of the black community at large. The video also contains clips of an interview with Marxist activist Melina Abdullah (organizer of the Black Lives Matter, Los Angeles chapter) whose comments are intended to build a suitably unfavorable narrative about American history so as to justify—and demonstrate sympathy for—violent riots in the United States. Throughout the film, the United States is referred to as a "system of oppression."

As a commander of young military professionals, all of whom have taken an oath to support and defend the Constitution, I became concerned that race-based identity politics would erode the trust and confidence these young people have in their country and in the Constitution. These same ideologically fueled narratives have continued to appear in various forums on base ever since. And, as will be seen throughout the book, my *base is not unique. These destructive narratives are spreading rapidly across US military bases and service academies everywhere.*

Suicide of the West

THERE ARE EFFORTS UNDERWAY TO DESTROY America's cultural identity and traditional values. That much is clear in Chapter 1. As a result of those efforts, many in our country are becoming ungrateful for America's founding principles. Partly, this is a result of the fact that it has become socially unacceptable to express gratitude or praise for the things that have made America exceptional. To praise American exceptionalism is to be labeled something mean—someone suffixed by a *"-phobic"* or an *"-ist,"* because to praise America is to belong to those vicious classes of people who are imperialists, racists, brutal capitalists, those who are oppressors, they who are everything that is wrong with society.

But those labels are lies.

It is reminiscent of a time not long ago when to praise even the quality of the roads in America was to earn one the label of "liar" in the Soviet Union and be sentenced to ten years in prison.[49] The same spirit has infiltrated American society. At the moment, we have a choice to not participate in that spirit. In his book *Suicide of the West,* Jonah Goldberg writes that the "corruption of the Miracle of Western Civilization…can only succeed when we willfully and ungratefully turn our back on the principles that brought us out of the muck of human history in the first place."[50]

The proliferation of Marxist narratives about America—or, at very least, narratives that Marxist activists utilize because they effectively divide the country—in combination with the collective sin of ingratitude, magnifies our divisions and resentments as a society. It makes us take America for granted. And to take America for granted means to not put in the requisite effort to preserve liberty. That is why when we see attempts to "reframe American history" in the manner that the *Times'* 1619 Project has, it should capture our attention and concern. These narratives are being used in our assemblies, as John Adams once said, to obtain influence "by noise, not sense. By meanness, not greatness. By ignorance, not learning. By contracted hearts, not large souls."[51]

The purpose of this chapter is to extend an invitation to examine America's founding philosophy so that those principles of which it is comprised might be better appreciated. Thus, we might begin to regain gratitude and turn back to that which unifies us as a nation. It is also hoped that in properly understanding America's founding philosophy, US military servicemembers might perceive its motivational relevance and more fully honor their oath to support and defend the Constitution.

The Real Reason for the American Revolution

On June 24, 1826, shortly before his death, Thomas Jefferson wrote a letter to Roger Weightman regretfully declining his invitation to participate in the fiftieth-anniversary celebration of the Declaration of Independence due to his declining health. The letter stands as Jefferson's last public testament in which he describes his views regarding the Declaration he authored—including a reference to the reasons for the American Revolution—and expresses the hope that Americans will retain an "undiminished devotion" to the rights of man expressed therein. Jefferson states, in pertinent part:

> The kind invitation I receive from you on the part of
> the citizens of the city of Washington, to be present
> with them at their celebration of the 50th anniversary of
> American independence; as one of the surviving signers
> of *an instrument pregnant with our own, and the fate of the
> world,* is most flattering to myself, and heightened by
> the honorable accompaniment proposed for the comfort
> of such a journey. [I]t adds sensibly to the sufferings of

sickness, to be deprived by it of a personal participation in the rejoicings of that day. [B]ut acquiescence is a duty, under circumstances not placed among those we are permitted to control. I should, indeed, with peculiar delight, have met and exchanged there congratulations personally with the small band, the remnant of that host of worthies, who joined with us on that day, *in the bold and doubtful election we were to make for our country, between submission or the sword; and to have enjoyed with them the consolatory fact, that our fellow citizens, after half a century of experience and prosperity, continue to approve the choice we made. [M]ay it be to the world, what I believe it will be, (to some parts sooner, to others later, but finally to all,) the Signal of arousing men to burst the chains, under which monkish ignorance and superstition had persuaded them to bind themselves, and to assume the blessings & security of self-government. [T]hat form which we have substituted, restores the free right to the unbounded exercise of reason and freedom of opinion. [A]ll eyes are opened, or opening, to the rights of man. .... [T]hese are grounds of hope for others. [F] or ourselves, let the annual return of this day forever refresh our recollections of these rights, and an undiminished devotion to them.*

I will ask permission here to express the pleasure with which I should have met my ancient neighbors of the City of Washington and of its vicinities, with whom I passed so many years of a pleasing social intercourse; an intercourse which so much relieved the anxieties of the public cares, and left impressions so deeply engraved in my affections, as never to be forgotten. With my regret that ill health forbids me the gratification of an acceptance, be pleased to receive for yourself, and those for whom you write, the assurance of my highest respect and friendly attachments.

Th. Jefferson[52] (Italics added)

At the time of America's founding, the most widespread claim to political legitimacy throughout Europe was "a form of the divine right of kings, that is to say, the assertion that God appoints some men, or some families, to rule and consigns the rest to be ruled."[53] As the authors of the 1776 Report affirm, the American founders rejected that claim. While England was not typical of other European absolutist monarchies—the divine right of kings being partly discredited as a result of the Glorious Revolution of 1688, which also overthrew James II and established parliamentary supremacy and a far-reaching Bill of Rights—its rule was deemed unjust, nonetheless. "As the eighteen charges leveled against King George in the Declaration of Independence make clear," the 1776 Report explains, "our founders considered the British government of the time to be oppressive and unjust."[54]

As social and political injustices imposed by the British crown mounted in the years leading to the American Revolution, colonists sent petitions to England proclaiming their grievances against the government, at times even petitioning the British people themselves to elect different members of Parliament who would be more open to compromise.[55] Many in the Congress hoped to achieve mutual agreement with the British government in order to secure the habit of self-government they had come to enjoy for the better part of a century.[56] Neither Parliament nor the king, however, were interested in compromise. Instead, as Ben Shapiro observes in his newest book *How to Destroy America In Three Easy Steps* (2020), they sought to increasingly restrict the rights of the colonists in the name of the "good."[57]

At last, as Jefferson explained in his letter to Weightman, the founders were compelled to choose between "submission or the sword." Their decision to take up the sword was not based merely upon the desire to replace the unjust, arbitrary government of one tyrant with that of another, however. They sought a new government, and, eventually, a republic—an historically fragile and short-lived form of government designed to be directed by the will of the people rather than the wishes of a single individual or a narrow class of elites.[58] Accordingly, they felt obligated to state a new principle of political legitimacy that would serve to underpin what would later become their new government. As they put it in the Declaration, a "decent respect to the opinions of mankind" required them to explain themselves and justify their revolution.[59] "They did not merely wish to assert that they disliked British rule and so were replacing it with something they liked better. They wished to state a justification for their actions, and for the government to which it would give birth, that is both *true* and *moral*: moral because it is faithful to the truth about things."[60]

In publicly declaring their justification, Jefferson hoped their decision would be a signal to the world to burst the chains by which it was bound, so that others, too, might "assume the blessings of security and self-government," and "restore the free right to the unbounded exercise of reason and freedom of opinion" that the American founders had themselves assumed and restored in America.

So, what did the founders offer as their justification? Upon what principles did Jefferson hope to signal to the nations of the earth that they, too, should assume the blessings of security and self-government?

The Declaration's most recognized lines contain the answer to these questions. Those lines begin:

> When in the Course of human events, it becomes necessary for one people to dissolve the political bands which have connected them with another, and to assume, among the Powers of the earth, the separate and equal station to which *the Laws of Nature and of Nature's God* entitle them, a decent respect to the opinions of mankind requires that they should declare the causes which impel them to the separation.

We hold *these truths to be self-evident, that all men are created equal, that they are endowed by their Creator with certain unalienable Rights, that among these are Life, Liberty, and the pursuit of Happiness.*—That to secure these rights, Governments are instituted among Men, deriving their just powers from the consent of the governed,—That whenever any Form of Government becomes destructive of these ends, it is the Right of the People to alter or to abolish it, and to institute new Government."[61] (Italics added)

The founding philosophy of the United States centers on these simple principles. The various unjust impositions of the British Government upon these principles justified the American Revolution and necessitated the formation of a new government that would honor and protect them. The principles are considered true because they are eternal—in other words, they are predicated upon a law that is "natural" and not created by man. And because natural law is not the creation of man, the rights stemming from such a law preexist government and cannot justly be infringed upon by government.

We now briefly consider these principles.

The Laws of Nature and of Nature's God

All men are created equal. This is not to say that every person is created or born with the same abilities, gifts, circumstances, opportunities, or proclivities, but that every person is equal before God and should *not* be treated as unequal before the law. Men and women of all races, religions, and political views are equally human—are all the same species and partakers of the same nature, endowed with the capacity to reason. It is in this principle—that "all men are created equal"—that the influence of Judeo-Christian values upon the founders becomes clearest, for to say that men are created equal is even at odds with some of the early Greek and Roman philosophers to whom the founders looked for their understanding of human nature and the purposes of government. In the language of Judeo-Christian scripture, all men are equally fallen and are reliant upon God for salvation. In political terms, all men are fallible.

To form a government on the premise that all men are created equal means that everyone is entitled to enjoy equality of citizenship. The fact that not every human enjoyed equal rights of citizenship at the country's inception—slaves, Native Americans, and women, for example—does not mean the principle is untrue. It means that America had yet to live up to its founding philosophy. That philosophy asserted what ought to be so—it was *prescriptive* and not *descriptive*. It informed Americans of a sacred obligation. The Declaration of Independence and Constitution were what Martin Luther King, Jr. described as "promissory notes to which every American was to fall heir."[62]

All men are endowed by their Creator with certain unalienable rights, that among these are life, liberty, and the pursuit of happiness. Whereas some believe that humans only enjoy such rights as are bestowed upon them by government, America's founding philosophy rejects this idea. The Declaration maintains that human rights are self-evident and result from a natural endowment belonging to every individual. No one, therefore, has an inherent right to rule or govern other sovereign individuals. Life itself is a gift, or endowment, of "nature and of nature's God." No one has an inherent right to take that from another, and therefore human beings have an inherent right to self-defense.

Every person is endowed with conscience and the capacity to reason. Liberty, therefore, is that natural right of each individual to think, believe, and act as he chooses consistent with right reason. Liberty means that a man's actions and the use of his possessions are subject to none other than his own will. Every man is free to govern his own life according to his conscience, so long as he does not interfere with another person's right to do likewise. Algernon Sidney (1623-1683), hero to John Adams and perhaps the least well-known English philosopher that was widely read in the American colonies, beautifully defined liberty in his *Discourses Concerning Government*. He said: "[I]f that which could be inherited was inherited by all, and it be impossible that a right of dominion over all can be due to everyone, then all that is or can be inherited by everyone is that exemption from the dominion of another, which we call liberty, and is the gift of God and nature."[63]

John Locke argued that in a state of nature, these rights to life and liberty preexist government. "The natural liberty of man is to be free from any superior power on earth," he explains, "and not to be under the will or legislative authority of man, but to have only the law of nature for his rule."[64] Because "all men are created equal," and all are equally endowed by their creator with life and liberty, every individual has inherent value. American philosophy holds that these truths are universal, regardless of whether governments honor them or unjustly violate the natural rights of their people.

That to secure these rights, governments are instituted among men. The purpose of government is to "secure," or protect, mankind's inalienable rights. This is the standard by which the justness of government is measured. Again, from where are the just powers of a government derived, or in what manner is its legitimacy determined? It is from the consent of the governed.

As individual liberty should be far-reaching, government should be limited in its scope. Attempts by governments to seek to control or limit a person's free exercise of thought, belief, or action are unjust. For a government to violate the individual rights of its citizens is for it to compromise its political legitimacy. At that point, it then becomes the right of the people to alter or abolish it. Admittedly, the older the United States gets the more it loses its bearings on its philosophical aspirations. What this all boils down to is that the preservation of man's free will—his ability to pursue proper being, the godly life, or what the declaration refers to as "happiness"—becomes the preeminent purpose for and obligation of man-made governments.

Despite what mainstream media, Big Tech, progressive politicians, and the creators of the 1619 Project would have you believe, *the facts of America's founding and the ideas and ideals of its founding philosophy are not partisan issues.*

America's founding philosophy and the principles described above are under attack in our country. The idea of a Creator, for example, is replaced with secularism and atheism. Equality before the law is replaced with forced equality of outcomes. Instead of celebrating our national achievements and progress, many demonize conservatives, whites, men, heterosexuals, Jews, Christians, and the rich, seeking to hold them accountable for evils and injustices of the past. The inherent value of the individual is attacked and replaced with value that is based upon group identity. Reason and the pursuit of objective truth are mocked, and postmodern subjectivity, ugliness, and criticism take their place. The liberties of many are trampled because of the insistence of a loud, angry, and sometimes violent minority. Self-defense is criminalized while destruction of others' personal property is permitted in the name of freedom, justice, and equality. Government overreach is now the rule rather than the exception.

To successfully decouple Americans from their founding philosophy is to leave them grasping at alternatives that are intended to reshape America's cultural narrative, identity, and values. The proliferation of these alternatives to America's founding philosophy only divides the country. Ironically, many now seek to dismantle America's founding philosophy only after the greatness of the American ideal has been recognized and adopted by countries all over the planet.

The near-universal appeal of the Declaration's wording and principles to America's founders is underscored in other important historical documents of this period. In his book *Rediscovering Americanism* (2017), Mark Levin explains:

> The Virginia Declaration of Rights was adopted on June 12, 1776, thereby predating the Declaration of Independence by a few weeks. It was principally drafted by George Mason, who would also play a significant role at the Constitutional Convention in 1787. The prominence of the Virginia Declaration is indisputable as some of its language was, in fact, borrowed by Jefferson in drafting the Declaration of Independence. Moreover, Benjamin Franklin, John Adams, and Samuel Adams used similar language in drafting future declarations of rights and constitutions for their own states.
>
> Section 1 of the Virginia Declaration provides: "That *all men are by nature equally free and independent and have certain inherent rights*, of which, when they enter into a state of society, they cannot by any compact, deprive or divest their posterity; namely, the *enjoyment of life and liberty*, with the means of *acquiring and possessing property*, and *pursuing and obtaining happiness and safety*." (Italics added)
>
> The Pennsylvania Declaration of Rights, adopted on August 16, 1776, and whose main author was Franklin, states, in Section 1: *"That all men are born equally free and independent, and have certain natural, inherent and inalienable rights, amongst which are, the enjoying and defending of life and liberty, acquiring, possessing and protecting property, and pursuing and obtaining happiness and safety."* (Italics added)

Article I of the Massachusetts Declaration of Rights, adopted in 1780, and whose authors included John Adams and Samuel Adams, states: *"All men are born free and equal, and have certain natural, essential, and unalienable rights;* among which may be reckoned the *right of enjoying and defending their lives and liberties; that of acquiring, possessing, and protecting property;* in fine, that of *seeking and obtaining their safety and happiness."* (Italics added)[65]

The appeal of the principles articulated in America's founding Rights documents, and formally codified as a consensus proclamation in the Declaration, quickly became more widespread. The American Declaration of Independence carried power as a symbol that was potentially global in extent, and it opened the eyes of all mankind leading to a new epoch in world history. Similar declarations were soon written around the world, just as Jefferson had foretold two weeks previous to his passing. It was as if America had become a city set upon a hill for all to observe.*

In his book *The Declaration of Independence: A Global History* (2017), David Armitage, professor of History at Harvard University, explains: "Even during [Jefferson's] lifetime, the Declaration had already become something more practical than a symbol: it provided the model for similar documents around the world that asserted the independence of other new states. By the time Jefferson called the Declaration 'an instrument pregnant with…the fate of the world' in 1826, it had already been joined by some twenty other declarations of independence from Northern and Southern Europe, the Caribbean, and Spanish America. Now, more than two centuries since 1776, over half the countries of the world have their own declarations of independence."[66] Many of these independence documents adopted

*In calling America "a city upon a hill," I am referring to John Winthrop's now famous 1630 sermon, which he wrote on the Atlantic Ocean aboard the flagship Arbella and delivered to his fellow settlers prior to their arrival in New England. In it he declared: "For we must consider that we shall be as a city upon a hill. The eyes of all people are upon us. So that if we shall deal falsely with our God in this work

specific phrases from the American Declaration, and those that did not, adopted the structure of the document for their own.[67]

A Silver Frame for the Golden Apple

The uniqueness of America's founding was not in the newness of the ideas it championed, but in the deliberate, free will instantiation of those ideas. This is described by Robert Reilly in his book *America on Trial: A Defense of the Founding* (2020). "The Founders not only declared the *inherited* principles of human equality, popular sovereignty, the requirement of consent, and the moral right to revolution," Reilly explains, "but, *for the first time in history*, instantiated them, put them into practice, producing a constitutional republic that was the product of deliberate and free choice."[68]

"It is one thing to discern and assert the true principles of political legitimacy and justice," the authors of the 1776 Report explain, but it is "quite another to establish those principles among an actual people, in an actual government, here on earth."[69] To that end, in May 1787, fifty-five delegates from twelve states (Rhode Island declined participation) traveled to Philadelphia to attend the Constitutional Convention. The Convention met with the aim of revising the existing Articles of Confederation. That weak confederacy was soon scrapped, however, and delegates spent nearly four months in deliberation. On September 17, at the conclusion of the Convention, thirty-nine delegates from eight states signed

---

we have undertaken, and so cause Him to withdraw His present help from us, we shall be made a story and a by-word through the world....We shall shame the faces of many of God's worthy servants, and cause their prayers to be turned into curses upon us *till we be consumed out of the good land whither we are going....But if our hearts shall turn away, so that we will not obey, but shall be seduced, and worship and serve other Gods, our pleasure and profits, and serve them; it is propounded unto us this day, we shall surely perish out of the good land whither we pass over this vast sea to possess it.*" (Italics added) See John Winthrop, "A Model of Christian Charity," in *A Library of American Literature: Early Colonial Literature, 1607-1675,* Edmund Clarence Stedman and Ellen Mackay Hutchinson, eds. (New York, NY: Charles L. Webster & Company, 1887), 307.

the Constitution of which James Madison was chief architect. Nine months later, on June 21, 1788, more than a decade after the Declaration of Independence was issued, the requisite ninth state ratified the document and a new frame of government was adopted, as Reilley put it, by "deliberate and free choice."

To understand the foundation of the Constitution, it is necessary to have first examined the laws of nature and of nature's God, as we have done above—there is a relationship between the two. Alexander Hamilton said that the rights named in both the Declaration and the Constitution "are not to be rummaged for, among old parchments," but rather "they are written, as with a sun beam, in the whole volume of human nature, by the hand of divinity itself."[70] Those laws of nature, and the inherent rights flowing therefrom, which are discoverable to humans by right reason, make plain the purposes and necessity for the American Republic.[71] The Constitution put into practice the American ideal and provided the method of operation of the new republic.[72] It remains the longest continually operating written constitution in all of human history.[73]

Lincoln understood this relationship between the Declaration and Constitution, describing it by way of analogy in a composition that is fortunately preserved in a fragment of text. He draws upon the King James translation of Proverbs 25:11—"A word fitly spoken is like apples of gold in pictures of silver"—describing the Declaration as "an apple of gold" and the Constitution as "the picture," or frame, of silver. The silver frame surrounds the golden apple, holding it in place and providing it necessary structure and support. "The picture was made, not to *conceal*, or *destroy* the apple; but to *adorn*, and *preserve* it," Lincoln observed.[74] (Italics in original) The Declaration's true principles, in Lincoln's view, are the word "fitly spoken." The overarching intent of his analogy is this: the preservation of the American ideal described in the Declaration was not possible without the Union and the Constitution.

Our military servicemembers swear an oath to support and defend the Constitution against all enemies, foreign and domestic.

In doing so, they should remember that the Constitution itself, sans the Declaration's universally true principles, is a hollow frame. In swearing the oath, these servicemembers commit to sacrifice all, if necessary, "that neither picture, or apple shall ever be blurred, or bruised or broken."[75]

The Declaration's Restful Finality

Some wrongly believe we can progress past the archaic ideas of America's founding philosophy. They believe the Constitution is outdated, and that it can and should be replaced. I know because I've had conversations with active-duty servicemembers with those views.

That there is opposition to the American ideal is unfortunate but not unexpected. In the end, there is opposition in all things—a kind of cosmic balance. Even this is determined by natural, eternal law. Regretfully, as a divided and increasingly polarized nation, we are our own worst enemy at present. The good news, however, is that we have a unique opportunity to act boldly, courageously, in the face of opposition to that which is just and true. For that, we can be grateful.

In July 1926, on the occasion of the 150th anniversary of the American Revolution, President Calvin Coolidge delivered a speech for the ages. Fittingly, his remarks were given in Philadelphia. In his speech, Coolidge boldly defended America's founding principles against an onslaught of progressivism—not coincidentally, this progressive impulse surged in the 1920s, the decade following the establishment of Communist Party USA—whose proponents believed the massive social and economic changes that had taken place in American life had invalidated those founding principles and required more modern theories of government be introduced to replace them.[76] Historian Wilfred McClay holds the view that Coolidge's speech "stands in the line of great presidential speeches from Jefferson to Lincoln, a reminder to Americans then and now of the exceptional character of their own revolution and of the enduring importance of liberty and equality as natural rights." Part of that speech follows:

> About the Declaration there is a finality that is exceedingly restful. It is often asserted that the world has made a great deal of progress since 1776, that we have had new thoughts and new experiences which have given us a great advance over the people of that day, and that we may therefore very well discard their conclusions for something more modern. But that reasoning can not be applied to this great charter. If all men are created equal, that is final. If they are endowed with inalienable rights, that is final. If governments derive their just powers from the consent of the governed, that is final. No advance, no progress can be made beyond these propositions. If anyone wishes to deny their truth or their soundness, the only direction in which he can proceed historically is not forward, but backward toward the time when there was no equality, no rights of the individual, no rule of the people. Those who wish to proceed in that direction can not lay claim to progress. They are reactionary. Their ideas are not more modern, but more ancient, than those of the Revolutionary fathers.[77]

Indeed, there is a restful finality to the principles of the American ideal. One cannot progress past an ideal that is both true and moral. Rather, we can and should strive to live up to that ideal—individually and unitedly.

The "great landmarks of the Declaration of Independence" to which Lincoln refers in the epigraph at the beginning of this chapter ought to be understood by every American, because they teach us truths about ourselves and about mankind. On August 17, 1858, Lincoln extended his plea to those who had been listening to "suggestions which would take away from the grandeur" of the "enlightened beliefs" of the founders.[78] Referring to the principles advocated by the founders in the Declaration of Independence, Lincoln declared: "This was their majestic interpretation of the economy of the Universe. This was their lofty, and wise, and noble understanding of the justice of the Creator to His creatures....to all His creatures, to the whole great family of man."[79]

Our brief discussion of the Declaration of Independence was necessary to extend anew Lincoln's entreaty "to come back"—an invitation as timely today as it has ever been. To discuss the Declaration is to remind readers of the timeless principles once believed by all Americans; principles by which they lived in hope and for which they died in sacrifice. It is intended to properly orient us to the peril our country faces even now as we abandon the Declaration's ideas and ideals. Our liberty is fragile, and yet so many somehow do not fear its loss.

PART II

MARXISM'S GOAL OF CONQUEST

AND A MIGHTY ANGEL took up a stone like a great millstone, and cast it into the sea, saying, Thus with violence shall that great city Babylon be thrown down, and shall be found no more at all.

John

CHAPTER 3

MARX, MARXISM, AND REVOLUTION, PART 1

If you know the enemy and know yourself, you need not fear the result of a hundred battles. If you know yourself but not the enemy, for every victory gained you will also suffer a defeat. If you know neither the enemy nor yourself, you will succumb in every battle.

Sun Tzu

I WAS GIVEN THE OPPORTUNITY *to attend what is considered the Defense Department's premier strategy school. It is affectionately—and self-approvingly—referred to as "the book-a-day club," because students read a book each day in preparation for a two-hour seminar in which lively dialogue ensues about the topics at hand. Throughout the year, we read the best writing on classical military theory, strategy, coercion, airpower history, international relations, irregular warfare, and military technology and innovation. It was, hands down, the best guided education I've ever had.*

In addition to the more than forty American students in the program—all majors and lieutenant colonels, and all potentially destined for leadership within the services—there were top officers from the Air Forces of Great Britain, Canada, Australia, and France. It was clear, nearly from day one, that each of us came to the table uniquely situated. We had all experienced life differently, had different upbringings, differ-ent career paths, and had somewhat different beliefs, preferences, and interests. Each student's uniqueness supplied a diversity of thought that made for enlightening discussion. We each brought a different lens to the texts we read, and, therefore, different interpretations of them. It is one of the reasons the academic year was so rewarding. Through practice, the group learned how to respectfully disagree with one another. We also learned what made a good argument, and what a strawman argument looked like. I'm sure each of us went home some days feeling like we just didn't articulate our thoughts very well. Sometimes, happily, we may have even experienced a change of perspective because of the compelling articulation of ideas by one of our classmates. We were grateful for one another.

The faculty at the school were also top-notch. I learned valuable les-sons from each of them. They were a wealth of experience and knowledge, and, yet, they seemed to be sensitive as to when they should interject and help steer a discussion by virtue of their insight, and when they should sit quietly and allow us all to fumble a bit. They were always available to the students at nearly all hours of the day and evening.

Interestingly, one of my professors seemed to me as skeptical of Amer-ican exceptionalism—perhaps even critical of it—as she was friendly toward Marxism. I will be the first to admit that she may not characterize her own views in that manner, but this was at least my perception based on my classes with her. The first time Marxism came up during the year was in her class. It was a class on the history of airpower during the Cold War, so the topic naturally came up on day one.

Before class, we read American diplomat George Kennan's now-fa-mous "Long Telegram," written in 1946 by Kennan from Moscow. Ken-nan's telegram was a response that sought to address questions asked of the State Department by the Treasury Department regarding recent Soviet behavior, such as its disinclination to endorse the International Monetary Fund and the World Bank. The telegram, which Kennan sent to Secre-tary of State James Byrnes, described a new plan for diplomatic relations with the Soviet Union that played a fundamental role in reshaping US foreign policy early in the Cold War. Of course, Kennan's assessment of Communist Soviet aims was that it posed a threat to liberty in the world. The details provided by Kennan seemed to me both honest and accurate. From what we now know about the twentieth century, Kennan's assessment of communist aims proved more than mere hyperbole.

The professor began class by asking if we thought Kennan's critique of communism was fair, or if it was merely American propaganda? It was a reasonable enough question, but the tenor of the question and mood of the subsequent discussion created an almost apologetic air toward Marxism and communism. It was as if some of the students sensed that Marxism had acquired some semi-protected or sacrosanct status within academia, or that it was intellectually honest to harbor some mildly obligatory skepticism toward America's narrative of communism, as if we had historically treated communism unfairly. We were learning to be thoughtful—critical—after all. ...

The Mirror of Mao's Cultural Revolution

IN 1966, SOMETHING TERRIBLE WAS HAPPENING in China that very few people in the West remember today because they were never taught about it in school. Banners bearing the slogans of Mao's cultural revolution appeared in the stands of a soccer field in China, where students had gathered to burn their books—all books, in fact, that did not have the sanctioned red cover:

"THE NEW SOCIETY WILL BE BUILT ON THE ASHES OF THE OLD!"

"BURN THE FEUDAL RELICS!"

"BURN THE SENTIMENTAL BOURGEOIS CULTURE!"

In the stands, sitting below the giant banner, a large group of younger students were clapping their hands and singing the Great Leader's song "Harden Our Hearts."[80]

Such is one of many remarkable recollections of Fan Shen, who was a professor at Rochester Community and Technical College in Minnesota in 2004 when he published his memoir *Gang of One*. He was a mere twelve years old when the Cultural Revolution began, and an enthusiastic participant in what he termed "cruel and destructive actions" against fellow Chinese citizens. The gripping account contained in his memoir bears an unsettling resemblance to the events we have seen unfold right here in the United States during the year 2020. If it had not been for the fact that Shen published his memoir back in 2004, one would be inclined to conclude that he falsely imposed themes from current events upon his stories relating to his own upbringing. Below is summarized what he recalls of his experiences as a young member of the Red Guard.

Revolutionaries, or "comrades" as they called themselves, were engaged in a relentless effort to expose and destroy "hidden enemies" of the revolution. By "hidden enemies" was meant citizens who would not overtly support the revolution. One of the ways they did that was by constantly changing language and altering the meaning of words, watching to see who would adopt the new vocabulary and who would reject it. Shen recollects that it became a "totally confusing war of words." One had to stay up on the current vocabulary to avoid indicating he was an enemy to the cause.

Forced equality, or equality of outcomes, became a social and cultural expectation, although it was never referred to that way—it was simply *equality*. Equality was a buzz word people could rally around. To sacrifice one's individuality and play a part in the revolution under the direction of the Great Leader gave one the sense he had become an equal.

After the revolution was under way, schools were shut down for extended periods of time, but the Party nevertheless allowed revolutionaries to gather with big letter signs for "endless rallies." Teachers were arrested if they were not supporters of the revolution. Their classrooms, vacant for months, became what young revolutionaries would use as their "headquarters," in which they would plot attacks and from which they carried them out.

The Chinese people became filled with hate while engaged in their desperate search to expose non-conformists. The "real fun" for these revolutionaries was at night when "struggle rallies" occurred. "Night after night, my friends and I sat in the front row and took in the drama," said Shen. "Our old math teacher, with dignified white hair, crying and begging for mercy; the superintendent of my school, a middle-aged woman, getting her face painted black by the Red Guards; and a senior student wearing a Red Guard armband collapsing and falling off the stage after tearfully shouting revolutionary slogans."[81] With the approach of summer, temperatures rose across Beijing, as did the intensity and attendance at the nightly struggle rallies, rising from dozens to many thousands of Chinese.* These rallies were a sea of red—red flags, red armbands, and red banners with slogans. Slogans were shouted at rallies:

"CONFESSION OR DEATH!"

"LONG LIVE THE RED TERROR!"

"LONG LIVE THE GREAT CULTURAL REVOLUTION!"

Rallies were purported to be "peaceful" but would inevitably descend into angry shouting and then violence, and "all carried concealed weapons like stones and sticks, just in case."[82] "We raised our fists and shouted with the loudspeakers," recalled Shen. "The shouting served its purpose. It got our blood boiling and we got more and more angry at the enemy sitting before us."[83]

During rallies, as elsewhere in the streets of the city, enemies of the revolution were forced to kneel and bow before the angry mob and were subject to compelled speech. To resist uttering the required "confessions," or apologies, was to risk violence, or worse.

---

* One should expect to see this same behavior across cities in the United States as temperatures rise during the late spring and early summer months of 2021.

So-called enemies either buckled under the weight of their fear and did what was required of them, or they resisted and became the subjects of senseless violence. Private and public property were likewise subject to the destructive march of the revolutionaries. Private residences were not only ransacked in the search to expose nonconformists but also to take their valuables. Public property was destroyed, and stores looted.

Day and night this tumult continued as propaganda teams spewed any combination of pejorative descriptions of their pretended enemies—the anti-revolutionaries who did not support the cause. This was all done to demonize one side in the conflict. It was a war, after all—a war Mao and his comrades created. Their demonization of the enemy was done purposefully so that illegal, violent acts against them were no longer unthinkable, but desirable. The calculated rhetoric employed against them had to generate the genuine belief that their opponent was evil, otherwise their brutality would be unconscionable. Those ends—the eradication of the evil other—justified any means.

Marxism thus became a religion itself.* It was, at least, an ideology—what Western intellectual Jordan Peterson aptly describes as a parasitical meme, or a parasite set upon a religious substructure. Once the evil archenemy is defined and discovered, Peterson explains, the "application of aggression, designed to obliterate the source of threat, appears morally justified, even required by duty."[84]

---

* In *Capitalism, Socialism, and Democracy* (1950), Joseph Schumpeter described the religious nature of Marxism: "In one important sense, Marxism is a religion. To the believer it presents, first, a system of ultimate ends that embody the meaning of life and are absolute standards by which to judge events and actions; and, secondly, a guide to those ends which implies a plan of salvation and the indication of the evil from which mankind, or a chosen section of mankind, is to be saved. We may specify still further: Marxist socialism also belongs to that subgroup which promises paradise on this side of the grave. The religious quality of Marxism also explains a characteristic attitude of the orthodox Marxist toward opponents. To him, as to any believer in a Faith, the opponent is not merely in error but in sin. Dissent is disapproved of not only intellectually but morally. There cannot be any excuse for it once the Message has been delivered." I am indebted to Dr. Ron Scott for pointing me to this reference.

Ultimately, the Chinese were caught in a fog of deception as lies were used deliberately to achieve "tactical victories." Culture was disrupted. Order replaced with chaos. The traditional social structure collapsed, and a new one, one that was the fruit of Mao's communism, was imposed upon millions.

Marx and Marxism

Marxism stands in stark contrast to the light and goodness of America's founding philosophy. American philosophy creates. It fosters individualism, voluntary cooperation, and freedom. It produces hope. Marxist ideology destroys and breeds fear and resentment. It strangles the free exchange of ideas and stifles free will. Since free will is the very essence of unfettered existence, it is no exaggeration to say that Marxism squelches existence. It was Marxism that fueled and guided Mao's Cultural Revolution. In Mao's mind, "Marxism must certainly advance," and "the basic principles of Marxism must never be violated."[85] The seeds of China's cultural destruction, however, were sown decades earlier, even before World War II, when Mao's communist revolution began to infect and spread like a cancer across China. After a protracted struggle, Mao's communists successfully installed a new regime when, in 1949, Chiang Kai-Shek and his Nationalists were exiled to the island of Taiwan.

Karl Marx, the founder of Marxism, however, was interested in revolutionizing more than merely one country. In fact, it is clear in Marx's writings that he was greatly interested in witnessing America's demise. To discuss Marxism, therefore, is to get a clearer picture of what is happening today in America specifically, and many nations in the West generally. America is walking the path many countries have walked before it during the twentieth century. It is a path fraught with danger. But what is happening at present is one thing, and what *will* happen if we continue to adopt Marxist ideology—whether wittingly or not—and behave in a manner consistent with its seditious and fratricidal impulse, is something different still. We will explore these ideas later in the book.

In my copy of *The Communist Manifesto* (Penguin Classics, 1967), there is in the front of the book a typical one-page biographical sketch of Karl Marx and Friedrich Engels. As a reader would expect, the biography is to-the-point, hitting those essential landmarks in Marx's life one might see in an obituary: the dates and places of his birth and death, and several grand highlights in between.

We learn that Marx was born in Trier in the Rhineland in 1818. He was the son of a Jewish lawyer who had converted to Christianity. As a student in Bonn and Berlin, Marx studied law and then philosophy. While a student, Marx joined the Young Hegelians, or Left Hegelians, an idealist following of German philosophy and the most radical of philosopher George W.F. Hegel's followers.

The group consisted largely of German intellectuals who wrote about Hegel's legacy and ideas during the decade following his death, and who rejected any of Hegel's ideas that seemed to them "anti-Utopian." Denying that Hegel's philosophy could be reconciled with Christianity or the existing State, the group mounted radical critiques of religion and the Prussian political system. Marx ended up being forced out of the University due to his radicalism, later participated in the 1848 revolution, and was then exiled with his family to London. He died in London in 1883.

History, however, is more complicated and always begins right in the middle of things. Any attempt to understand Marx or *The Manifesto* beginning merely with his own story is, therefore, incomplete. As American historian Wilfred McClay observes:

> It doesn't matter where you choose to start the story; there is always something essential that came before, some prior context that is assumed. This is why the past can't be divided up into convenient self-contained units, with clear and distinct beginnings and endings, much as we might wish it were otherwise. Instead, the spec-

tacle that lies before us when we gaze backward is more like a sprawling, limitless river with countless mingling branches and tributaries, stretching back to the horizon. Like a river, time's restless force pushes ever forward, but its beginnings lie far back, extending far beyond what we can see, fading into the mists of time at the edges of lands beyond our knowing.[86]

A proper understanding of Marx and Marxism, then, inevitably pre-dates the birth of Marx himself. For one, communism and socialism pre-date Marx; but for another, certain men and ideas had a tremendous influence on Marx's thinking that must not be overlooked. Hegel, mentioned in the brief biographical sketch above, is one of several important influences to briefly discuss. We shall talk more about Hegel, but first, we go back to 1776.

Enlightenment and Illuminists

At the same time the founders were inspired to create the greatest declaration of rights in human history—the Declaration of Independence—and thereafter establish a limited form of government ensuring the preservation of individual liberty for the citizens of the nascent American State, another group of men were inspired by a revolutionary spirit to organize themselves across the world.

In 1776, a private reading club was formed in Bavaria (roughly modern Germany) by an obscure academic by the name of Adam Weishaupt. The private club, referred to by Weishaupt himself as a secret society, lasted officially for little more than a decade (1776-1787). Nonetheless, for its eleven years of existence this amazingly successful secret society, which came to be known as the Bavarian Order of the Illuminati, had managed to penetrate nearly every court in the Holy Roman Empire and had initiated some of the most intelligent and influential adherents of the Enlightenment, from princes and high-ranking bureaucrats to university professors.[87]

When encountering the word "Illuminati," it is perhaps necessary to temporarily suspend any healthy skepticism one may have acquired, whether from fictionalized Dan Brown novels or elsewhere on the internet. The name has been usurped, used, reused, and abused for a long time to mean different things by different groups of people. Its mere mention is to even summon disrepute. But there was, in fact, a secret society formed at this time which was called the Order of the Illuminati (*Illuminatenordens*). We are not interested in conspiracy theory, only history; in this case, the history of a group of co-conspirators whose political and social aims influenced Karl Marx.

At its founding, the Order consisted of an original membership of five men, considered by Weishaupt to be worthy of being admitted into his mysteries and upon whom he conferred "the highest degree" of honors or rights.[88] He called his inductees *Areopagites* (presumably in the sense that they comprised a tribunal, or council of Judges, as did those ancient Athenian senators who met at the Areopagus, or the rock outcropping the Romans later referred to as Mars Hill), installed himself as their chief, and referred to the small brotherhood as *The Order of Illuminees*.

As mentioned, the Order was secret, but it was also hierarchical and modeled on the Jesuits, a religious order founded by Spaniard Ignatius of Loyola and sanctioned by Pope Paul III in 1540, and which was ostensibly suppressed on a worldwide basis in 1773, following a decree of Pope Clement XIV. Instead of being a religious order, however, the Illuminati sought to rise above religion, which necessitated the abolition of religion itself.

Calling themselves *Perfectionists* (or *Perfectibilists;* Ger. *Perfectibilisten*), the secret society had a certain conception of human nature, of the perfectibility of man, and believed that it was the traditions of the corrupt state, and of the Church in particular, that stood in the way of mankind's march to earthly perfection. Some believed that the ascent to enlightenment was to approach the perfection of the Father of Enlightenment, or light-bearer *Lucifer*, who had been cast out of heaven by an unjust Patriarch. The enlightened man's obligation, then, was to rebel against his unelected masters.* They were, in a word, Utopians.

During the eighteenth century, the idea of a "glorious revolution" born from such enlightenment appears to have attained widespread acceptance throughout Europe. The rhetoric of the age was *critical*; the Age of Enlightenment was, after all, also known as the "age of criticism." Prussian philosopher Immanuel Kant (1724-1804) explained it well:

> Our age is, in especial degree, the age of criticism, *and to criticism everything must submit*. Religion through its sanctity, and law-giving through its majesty, may seek to exempt themselves from it. But they then awaken just suspicion, and cannot claim the sincere respect which reason accords only to that which has been able to sustain the test of free and open examination.[89] (Italics added)

The "imminent revolution of the human mind," promulgated by Weishaupt's Illuminists, coincided with the *Comte de Mirabeau's* (1749-1791) doctrine of a coming secular upheaval and universal revolution. Mirabeau's view was that Prussia was the most likely place for the start of the revolution, with the "German Illuminists as its probable leaders."[90] His sense was keen and reasonable, for within several years of its establishment, the Bavarian Order of the Illuminati had grown from hundreds to thousands.

---

*In a similar vein, Saul Alinsky dedicated his *Rules for Radicals* (1971), Alinsky's impassioned counsel to young radicals on how to effect social change, to Lucifer: "Lest we forget at least an over-the-shoulder acknowledgement to the very first radical: from all our legends, mythology, and history (and who is to know where mythology leaves off and history begins—or which is which), the first radical known to man who rebelled against the establishment and did it so effectively that he at least won his own kingdom—Lucifer."

Besides the initial contemporary accounts of John Robison (1739-1805) and ex-Jesuit Abeé Augustin de Barruel (1741-1820), studies about the Illuminati were largely neglected in the English language until the last half-century. Germany, the birthplace of the Order, witnessed a renaissance in Illuminati studies beginning in the late 1950s, and the translation of source documents has since led to a renewed interest in the topic in the English-speaking world. From translations of period German, French, and Italian texts that survived, including from the writings of Weishaupt and some of those closest to him, scholars have assembled a patchwork of what they believe to have been the aims of the Order:

1. The abolition of monarchy and all ordered government;
2. The abolition of private property and of inheritance;
3. The abolition of patriotism;
4. The abolition of the family (i.e. of marriage and all morality, and the institution of the communal education of children); and
5. The abolition of all religion[91]

Each of these traditions and institutions stood as barriers to the glorious revolution, to the remaking of the world in the image of the enlightened man. The opposition they posed necessitated their removal. In addition to these, Illuminists also believed in technocratic rule despite all their rhetoric about equality.[92] The ties between these aims and those of Marxism will become apparent. Weishaupt, through his Order of the Illuminati, is clearly one of the Enlightenment era founts from which sprang communism. As author Terry Melanson observes: "Even before the various labels were defined in the early 19th century, Weishaupt preached to his disciples the restructuring of society along lines similar to socialism and communism, tinged with elements of nihilism and anarchism."[93]

But the Illuminati's aims were fractured when scandal broke. Just less than a decade after the formation of the Order, the Elector of Bavaria, Duke Karl Theodor, issued an edict on June 22, 1784, outlawing all "fraternal societies clandestine and unapproved," also stating: "His Electoral Highness has decided not to tolerate them in his State, whatever their designation and interior constitutions."[94] In his first edict, the Illuminati were never mentioned by name. A second edict came in March of the following year reiterating the ban; this time, however, the edict specifically mentioned the Illuminati and Freemasonry, leaving "no room for evasion." It read, in part:

> We, Karl Theodor, by the grace of God, Count-Palatine of the Rhine (*et al.*)…have been deeply affected and displeased to learn that *the various Lodges of so-called Freemasons and Illuminati*, who are still in our States, have taken so little heed of our General Prohibition issued on June 22nd of last year against all fraternal societies clandestine and unapproved, as to *not only continue to hold meetings in secret, but even to raise funds and recruit new members, seeking to further increase the already large number of adepts.* We had deemed this Society, very much degenerated and of primitive institution, too suspect both as regards to religious concerns and from a social and political point of view, so that we could no longer tolerate it in our States…. [W]e command that all authorities must execute our orders exactly and secretly inform us of any disobedience."[95] (Italics added)

Neither the Duke of Bavaria, nor those other royal parties who co-signed the edict, were sure just how extensive the alliance was between the Illuminists and the Freemasons.* What they were certain about, however, was that, despite outlawing these and other

---

* Despite the Duke's uncertainty, the alliance between these two factions is well-documented. On July 16, 1782, a conference was convened at Wilhelmsbad that was probably the most significant event of the era pertaining to any official coalition between secret society factions. It was convoked by Ferdinand, Duke of Brunswick, Grand Master of the Order of Strict Observance (a lodge of the Freemasons). Present

secret societies, they seemed to be continuing to meet, fundraise, and recruit new members. The ruling class therefore harbored great concerns over their aims. They were shrewd enough themselves to understand that even if they outlawed an ideology, they could not guarantee its eradication.

As the ruling class might have expected, in response to that second edict, which explicitly banned the Order, the Illuminists soon went to the underground. Their debatable disappearance left in its wake a specter that haunted governments throughout Europe, causing monarchs to continue to fear their plans. Whether the Order's existence had remained public, become entirely private, or simply chose to go by other names, Weishaupt had long believed that concealment was a chief strength of the Order. "The great strength of our Order lies in its concealment," Weishaupt explained. "[L]et it *never appear in any place in its own name, but always covered by another name*, and another occupation."[96] (Italics added) Weishaupt also said: "Yes, Princes and nations shall disappear from off the face of the Earth. Yes, the time shall come when man shall acknowledge no other law but the Great Book of Nature. This revolution shall be the work of secret societies and that is one of our grand mysteries."[97] Not surprisingly, some historians believe that this underground secret society fueled the French Revolution.[98]

were delegates from Upper and Lower Germany, Holland, Russia, Italy, France, and Austria. The Order of the Illuminati was represented by the Baron Von Knigge at the same conference. Melanson references the controversial Nesta Webster: "It was not until the Congrès de Wilhelmsbad that the alliance between Illuminism and Freemasonry was finally sealed," she wrote. "What passed at this terrible Congress will never be known to the outside world, for even those men who had been drawn unwittingly into the movement, and now heard for the first time the real designs of the leaders, were under oath to reveal nothing. One such honest Freemason, the Comte de Virieu, a member of the Martiniste Lodge at Lyons, returning from the Congrès de Wilhelmsbad could not conceal his alarm, and when questioned on the "tragic secrets" he had brought back with him, replied: 'I will not confide them to you. I can only tell you that all this is very much more serious than you think. The conspiracy which is being woven is so well thought out that it will be, so to speak, impossible for the monarchy and the Church to escape from it.' From this time onwards, says his biographer, M. Costa de Beauregard, 'the Comte de Virieu could only speak of Freemasonry with horror.'" Quoted in Melanson, *Perfectibilits*, 22-23.

To Weishaupt, the ends Illuminists pursued justified any means. What were those ends? In addition to the five aims—really lines of effort—set out above, they were simply these: the introduction of a "worldwide moral regime which would be under their control in every country," which would provide a council that "would decide on all matters concerning pardons, appointments and promotions, as well as rejections *sine appelatione ad principem*. This would give it the unlimited right...to pronounce final judgment over the honesty and usefulness of an individual."[99] The ends, therefore, justified calling for revolution and the violent overthrow of the existing social and political order. From one of the surviving documents of the Order:

> *[T]he grand art of rendering any revolution whatsoever certain*—is to enlighten the people—and to enlighten them is, insensibly *to turn public opinion to the adoption of those changes which are the given object of the intended revolution.*
>
> When that object cannot be promulgated without exposing him that has conceived it to public vengeance, he must know how to propagate his opinion in Secret Societies.
>
> *When the object is an universal Revolution*, all the members of these societies, aiming at the same point, and aiding each other, *must find means of governing invisibly*, and without any appearance of violent measures, not only the higher and more distinguished class of any particular state, but men of all stations, of all nations, and of every religion—Insinuate the same spirit everywhere—In silence, but with the greatest activity possible.
>
> *This empire once established* by means of the union and multitude of the adepts, *let force succeed to the invisible power. Tie the hands of those who resist;* subdue and stifle wickedness in the germ.[100] (Italics added)

One point above is remarkable, and bears repeating.

"*The grand art* [emphasis added] of rendering any revolution whatsoever certain…" is "to turn public opinion to the adoption of those changes which are the given object of the intended revolution."

It is a brilliant strategy; one that, if achieved, would make any revolution a *fait accompli*. Illuminists referred to this subversive indoctrination as "enlightening the people." However, it is really nothing more than the corruption of human thought, the disruption of traditional culture, and the dismantling of social norms. Keep those ideas in mind because they will appear again.

Finally, we return to where we ended the previous section; specifically, to the idea that a proper understanding of Marx and Marxism pre-dates the birth of Marx himself. That Weishaupt and his companions directly influenced communists and socialists throughout Europe is undeniable, but we have yet to consider the individuals who were the bridge between the Illuminists and Marx. Tracing through all the various progeny of the Order is well beyond the scope of this work and unnecessary. We shall briefly consider only several.

Buonarroti, Malthus, Hegel

A direct line of influence from the Illuminati to the French Revolution to the Communist League of the Just is realized in a single individual—Filippo Michele Buonarroti (1761-1837). The Italian-born revolutionary was a preacher of socialism and communism who claimed: "[Jean-Jacques] Rousseau was [his] master."

At the age of seventeen, coincidentally the same year that Rousseau died, Buonarroti enrolled at the University of Pisa and studied law. It was there that he was introduced to Rousseau's work, which would become a lifelong passion for him. "The dogmas of equality and of popular sovereignty inflamed my being," he wrote.[101] After his schooling, Buonarrati became a Freemason. Historian Carlo Francovich asserts that he later joined the Florence lodge of the Illuminati in 1786, though he stakes his claim upon an unverifiable single source. Buonarrati biographer Elizabeth Eisenstein is cautious of Francovich's assertion, while herself noting that while Buonarroti's "initiation into Weishaupt's order remains conjectural, his later familiarity with it is certain and was to be of paramount importance in his future development."[102]

In 1789, with the onset of the French Revolution, Buonarrati found his calling and true purpose in life, writing: "I had been waiting a long time for the signal, [and] it was given."[103] He became editor of a revolutionary Corsica paper, *Giornale Patriottico di Corsica*, and a friend of Baron de Bassus, one of the highest ranking and most influential members of the Illuminati. Both men were enthralled with the Revolution. By March 1793, Buonarrati had moved to France, become a French citizen, and befriended Maximilien Robespierre, for whom he had great respect throughout his life. In early 1794, he joined Robespierre's younger brother, Augustine, Napoleon Bonaparte, and the French Army on the Italian Riviera during the Reign of Terror.[104]

That same year, Buonarrati remained keenly engaged. He was given governance of the city of Oneglia, a town in his home country of Italy, instituted a Revolutionary Dictatorship, established a *Comité de Surveillance*, and a Revolutionary Tribunal, which, he assured General André Masséna by letter, allowed him to "guillotine the traitors from within."[105] He established pedagogical institutions to "enlighten" the citizens with the socialist dogma of Rousseau, and illegally confiscated land belonging to members of the noble class. One such noble from whom Buonarrati stole land, was, apparently, a Genoese aristocrat who was well-connected to the revolutionary government, and who had Buonarrati arrested. Buonarrati was sentenced to serve time at Du Plessis prison in Paris, during which time he met and befriended François-Noël (Gracchus) Babeuf

(1760-1797), a radical French socialist, revolutionary, and journalist, who was also known as the "First Revolutionary Communist."

Following his release from prison on October 9, 1795, Buonarroti was resolved to destroy the privilege of those who had benefited from the Revolution and, thus, advocated for the abolition of all private property to ensure equality for all of France—a pursuit for a kind of Rousseauian radical egalitarianism. He joined the Pantheon Society, which included remnants of the Jacobin Club, and plotted with Babeuf in the Conspiracy of Equals, an attempted (and failed) coup d'etat in France in May 1796. Babeuf was later executed for his role in the Conspiracy, and Buonarrati spent the next nine years in prison.[106]

Towards the end of his life, after spending years creating secret societies in France, Switzerland, and Italy, Buonarrati wrote what would be his most lasting and influential legacy: *Conspiration pour l'Egalité dite de Babeuf, suivie du procès auquel elle donna lieu, et des pieces justificatives, etc.* ("Babeuf's Conspiracy of Equals, followed by the trial of which it gave rise, with supporting documents, etc."). It was published first in Brussels in 1828, and then in Paris in 1830. Soon after, it was translated into English, German, Italian, and Russian.[107] Eisenstein observes that Buonarrati's seminal work "injected a spirit of revolutionary messianism into continental socialism, founded a long-lived historical school and created a martyrology that inspired many of the future men of 1848."[108]

Among the "future men" to whom Eisenstein was referring are none other than Karl Marx and Friedrich Engels, who possessed and read Buonarrati's work. According to journalist and author Eugene H. Methvin, "Europe's utopian communists, radicals, reformers, and revolutionaries of the 1830s and 1840s passed Buonarrati's book from hand to hand."[109]

In 1847, Marx's and Engels' Communist Correspondence Committee combined with the League of the Just—a so-called Christian Communist international revolutionary organization that had been formed in Paris in 1836 and was based on Buonarrati's teachings—to form the Communist League.

Two other bridge-makers between the Illuminists and Marx are Thomas Robert Malthus (1766-1834) and Georg W.F. Hegel (1770-1831), whose writings were known to and influential in the life of Marx. The former was an English country curate whose father was friends with Rousseau, who, as mentioned, was a philosophical figurehead for Illuminists. Malthus had a major influence on Charles Darwin's theories about evolution and, being concerned about the mismatch between population growth and resources, was a proponent of population control and what became the eugenics movement.[110]

In 1798, Malthus put his thoughts to paper in his *Essay on the Principle of Population*, which became widely read and has been debated ever since. His grim forecasts based upon the population-resources mismatch called for "periodic wars, famines or plagues to 'reduce the surplus population,' or we would soon be standing shoulder to shoulder."[111] Malthus further promoted "hygienically unsound practices amongst impoverished populations," believing "that the 'undesirable elements' of the human herd could be naturally culled by various maladies. The spread of disease could be further assisted through discriminative vaccination and zoning programs."[112] Malthus' work seems to have directly influenced Marx's ideas about "capital."[113]

Hegel, who was born in Stuttgart Germany, was friends with, mentored by, and read the writings of members of the Illuminati. He created what came to be known as the "Hegelian dialectic," a method of philosophical argument which relies upon a purposely contradictory cross-examination of opposing sides (thesis and antithesis) that produces a synthesis that is theoretically truer than either of the first two determinations.[114]

Hegel's philosophy went beyond a mere method of argument or a general set of principles for logical thought, however; instead, it was a worldview. For Hegel, the idealistic dialectic drove even the evolution of history itself. According to British-American economist and historian Antony Sutton, "For Hegelians, the State is almighty and seen as 'the march of God on earth.' Indeed, a State religion. *Progress in the Hegelian State is through contrived conflict: the clash of opposites makes for progress. If you can control the opposites, you dominate the nature of the outcome.*"[115] (Italics added)

Marx's writings are replete with references to Hegel, both affirmative and critical. And though Marx's views are admittedly more materialistic, Hegel's notion that history conforms to and unfolds in a dialectical pattern permeates Marx's narrative of history as a perpetual clash of opposites between two classes: the oppressors and the oppressed.

Thus, the works of Buonarrati, Malthus, and Hegel manifest the unmistakable potential for the transmission of Adam Weishaupt's views to Karl Marx. The degree to which Marx drew upon and resonated with Weishaupt's views—or assimilated his aims—can be gleaned from what follows in the next chapter. We are therefore left to explore any relationships between the social and political aims of the Illuminati, as well as other European secret societies of the late-eighteenth and early-nineteenth centuries, and the social and political aims of Marxism.*

---

* I acknowledge the apparent restrictedness of this genealogy of Marxist thought. Others (Lenin included) point to several, albeit related, influences on Marx's writings: English political economy, French utopian socialism, republicanism and radicalism, and German idealist philosophy, for example. My narrative is not exhaustive, nor is it meant to be. And while it touches upon these other influences, it is intended to convey primarily that the schemes of secret societies to overthrow governments, religion, and the family, are a driving force in Marxism.

CHAPTER 4

MARX, MARXISM, AND REVOLUTION, PART 2

The Manifesto is, as the historical record attests, an incitement to totalitarian ambitions whose results were even bloodier than those inspired by Mein Kampf. In it Marx announced the doom of free market societies, declared the liberal bourgeoisie to be a "ruling class" and the democratic state its puppet, summoned proletarians and their intellectual vanguard to begin civil wars in their own countries, and thereby launched the most destructive movement in human history.

David Horowitz

BACK TO KENNAN'S LONG TELEGRAM. ....*As I said at the beginning of the previous chapter, the professor began class by asking if we thought Kennan's critique of communism was fair, or if it was merely American propaganda?*

At the time, I was largely ignorant of the subject, as were, I'm sure, most of the students in the room. We had merely done the day's reading. I do not remember the rest of the class discussion that day. All I remember is that my interest was piqued. But I also was somewhat disturbed—displeased with our apparent required but burgeoning skill to criticize everything we read, whether or not we were in possession of any substantive, alternative facts or narratives worthy of contribution for serious consideration. To criticize seemed a necessary tool in one's education, but perhaps there was a healthy way to go about it as well as a destructive way. What was the intent of critique, anyway? Was it to acquire understanding? Was it a design to lead us to a particular, desired perspective? Or worse, was it merely a misleading, lofty but arrogant type of self-aggrandizement?

I soon found out that this same professor was assigned to be my thesis advisor, and I had semi-frequent interactions with her throughout the year. She was as gregarious and likeable as anyone you would meet. I well remember the day when students were scheduled to present our thesis topics and methodology before a group of faculty and peers. My thesis topic was related to organizational culture, and I had personally found the work of Jordan Peterson exciting and insightful; specifically, his earlier, lesser-known work, Maps of Meaning: The Architecture of Belief, *which was recommended to me by another professor as a deep and thorough investigation of the human psyche, beliefs, and culture. Months earlier, the opening lines of the Preface of that work captured my attention:*

> *Something we cannot see protects us from something we do not understand. The thing we cannot see is culture, in its intrapsychic or internal manifestation. The thing we do not understand is the chaos that gave rise to culture. If the structure of culture is disrupted, unwittingly, chaos returns. We will do anything—anything—to defend ourselves against that return.*

I decided to study the book in greater depth and to explore ways I might use the model explained in Peterson's work as a framework for my own research. During my short presentation to the group of faculty and students, I explained that I would be using Peterson's 1999 work to frame my research into organizational culture, and further explained why I liked the model he presented in his book. I became distracted, however, as I watched one professor lean over and whisper in the ear of my thesis advisor. It was not subtle. The whisperer then interrupted my presentation with a question to my advisor in front of the entire group:

"Do you want to tell him, or do you want me to?"

My advisor then informed me—and the rest of my peers—that referencing Jordan Peterson for my research was "like referencing Hitler." As most readers know, however, Jordan Peterson is nothing like Hitler. I was left speechless. My best guess was that neither of these two had ever spent much time reading what Peterson had written.

But mine was not the only dismaying juncture of the morning.

During another student's thesis presentation in that same meeting, one of these two professors corrected the presenter's speech, cautioning her—and all of us—to not use words such as "man," or "men," or "mankind," or, as was the case in this student's presentation, "manned spaceflight." Such terms were inappropriately exclusive, and, therefore, offensive, and should be avoided.

From that day forward I began learning more about what I had seen. I was not the only student bothered by the experience. I learned that Peterson, himself a professor of clinical psychology at the University of Toronto, had become famous for a number of reasons during the past several years, not the least of which was his public stand against compelled speech within the University. A number of YouTube videos of Peterson explaining his stance went viral. About that time, he published his much better-known work, 12 Rules for Life: An Antidote to Chaos, which is a more digestible synthesis of some of the ideas he had introduced in his 1999 work, and which, he explains, was spurred by a popular Quora post.

Peterson's many lectures and videos have been about a variety of topics, such as human nature, psychology, and culture. They generally, therefore, have bearing upon politics, religion, and what Peterson often refers to as proper Being. Perhaps his greatest contribution, however, is his explication of the psychology and methods of totalitarian regimes, and his harsh critique of Marxism and the brutality of communist states during the twentieth century. He is as fierce an opponent of Marxist ideology as anyone (and equally as critical of Hitler, by the way), and of all strongmen suffused with the totalitarian impulse. And, of course, *to be such an opponent leads Peterson to critique many other social and cultural phenomena we see manifest in modern society, which arise from the kind of dictatorial control sought for by evil and conspiring men in the twentieth century. He therefore addresses—and attacks—postmodernism, political correctness, radical feminism, progressivism, and the concept of safe spaces on university campuses. He can be brutal, but he is always brutally honest. And his voice resonates with literally millions because there are millions of honest people who are trying to understand what is taking place in the complex world in which they live. It is no wonder that leftists view Peterson as a mortal enemy—a kind of political archnemesis.*

My experiences at school and my subsequent introduction to Peterson's work heightened my interest in Marxism. The library at Maxwell Air Force Base has a tremendous section on Marx, Marxism, and communist revolutions, and I spent a lot of time there during the months that followed. I read the Communist Manifesto, Department of Defense (DoD) manuals from the Cold War that were once distributed to inform servicemembers about the lurking threat of communism, and other interesting works that were written decades ago and have long since been lost to society's memory, if they were ever known at all. It was but the beginning of far more research into the matter. The more I learned about it all, the more I saw it all around me. The critic would say that's simply natural, and that my perceptions are merely shaped and influenced by my beliefs.

That's true.

What is also true is that not all beliefs and interpretations of the world are equally valid.

The Young Marx

MARX'S REVOLUTIONARY FERVOR was deep-seated and emotional, stemming at least in part from a spiritual drive for vengeance upon God that shows up in his earliest writings. By the mid-1830s, just several years after Adam Weishaupt's death (1830), the teenage Marx was becoming a prolific writer. His abandonment of his Christian upbringing and resultant anger is on display in his poetry. In his early poem "Invocation of One in Despair," Marx writes of his determination to take revenge on God:

> So a god has snatched from me my all
> In the curse and rack of Destiny.
> All his worlds are gone beyond recall!
> *Nothing but revenge is left to me!*
>
> On myself *revenge I'll proudly wreak,*
> *On that being, that enthroned Lord,*
> Make my strength a patchwork of what's weak,
> Leave my better self without reward!
>
> *I shall build my throne high overhead,*
> *Cold, tremendous shall its summit be.*
> For its bulwark—superstitious dread,
> For its Marshall—blackest agony.[116] (Italics added)

His pronouncement that he "shall build [his] throne high overhead" appears to be an allusion to Lucifer's aspiration, as portrayed by Isaiah: "How are you fallen from heaven, O Lucifer, Son of the Morning! How are you cut down to the ground, You that weakened the nations! For you have said in your heart: 'I will ascend into heaven, I will exalt my throne above the stars of God; I will also sit on the mount of the congregation on the farthest sides of the North; I will ascend above the heights of the clouds, I will be like the Most High.'"[117]

In a letter to his father, dated November 10, 1837, Marx described what can only be interpreted as inner turmoil, a state of despair: "A curtain was fallen," Marx explained, "my holiest of holies was ripped apart, and new gods had to be set in their place....A true unrest has taken mastery of me and I will not be able to calm the excited spirits until I am in your dear presence."[118]

In his poem "The Pale Maiden," Marx employs the lyrical voice of a young woman who abandons her love of Christ and meets a dreadful end. He writes, in part:

All peace of mind is flown,
The Heavens have sunk.
The heart, now sorrow's throne,
Is yearning-drunk.

And when the day is past,
She kneels on the floor,
Before the holy Christ
A-praying once more.

But *then upon that form*
Another encroaches,
To take her heart by storm,
'Gainst her self reproaches.

Thus heaven I've forfeited,
I know it full well.
My soul, once true to God,
Is chosen for hell.[119] (Italics added)

The changes in the young Marx had given his father cause for concern. In a letter dated March 2, 1837, Marx's father explains that despite having long hoped his son's name would someday be "of great repute," none of his son's "earthly" accomplishments could truly make a father happy. "Only if your heart remains pure and beats humanly and if no demon is able to alienate your heart from better feelings, only then will I be happy," he wrote.[120]

Abandoning God and associating with Satan is a common theme in Marx's poetry. In "The Fiddler," Marx again speaks in the lyrical voice:

How so! I plunge, plunge without fail
My blood-black saber into your soul.
That art God neither wants nor wists,
It leaps to the brain from Hell's black mists.

Till heart's bewitched, till senses reel:
With Satan I have struck my deal.
He chalks the signs, beats time for me,
I play the death march fast and free.[121]

One of Marx's biographers, Robert Payne, explains that the stories Marx told can be taken as allegories for his own life, not mere abstractions. If his poetry might somehow be construed not as a reflection of his own feelings, but simply as artistic expression, however, then his own statements clear up the matter. Marx declared: "I long to take vengeance on the One Who rules from above," and, referencing communists: "We make war against all prevailing ideas of religion, of the state, of country, of patriotism. The idea of God is the keynote of a perverted civilization. It must be destroyed."[122]

Marx displayed affinity for the words of Mephistopheles in Goethe's *Faust*, and quoted them in his own work *The Eighteenth Brumaire of Lois Bonaparte*: "All that exists deserves to perish."[123] In *Faust*, Satan is called the spirit that denies everything, and this is precisely what became of Marx's attitude. He writes in September 1843, just five years before *The Manifesto* is published, that "what we have to accomplish at present" is the "ruthless criticism of all that exists."[124]

At the same time that Marx was creating poetry, he took interest in the Young Hegelian circle in Berlin in the summer of 1837. There, Bruno Bauer became his mentor and remained a dominant force in Marx's intellectual development until at least 1843.[125] Bauer believed that true reform required not merely the elimination of God, but an end to Christian culture.[126] In 1841, Marx and Bauer jointly planned a new journal that was to be called *The Archives of Atheism*. As Marx said in his university thesis, he was intent upon philosophy taking its stand against "all heavenly and earthly Gods who do not acknowledge human self-consciousness as the highest divinity."[127]

Like other Young Hegelians, Marx believed that the means by which the transition to a new epoch of human history was to be secured was "the will" in the form of "criticism." Young Hegelian "will" was intent upon dismantling the claims of Christianity, which Marx critiqued as limited in scope, and insisted they go further, believing the state and civil society were at least equally as deserving of criticism.[128] But, although he and other Young Hegelians were careful to ensure their criticism was not perceived as a direct attack upon the Christian state, they were shocked when in 1843 the government shut down their main newspaper, the *Rheinische Zeitung*, as well as other opposition publications. The paper had been established by leading liberals of the Rhineland who were campaigning for representative government and liberal reforms.

Marx could not help but wonder why there was so little opposition to the government's suppression of the free press. In 1830, when the last Bourbon king, Charles X, had attempted a similar suppression of the liberal press in France, it caused a revolution. Why not in Prussia, Marx wondered?

The Communist Manifesto—Its Origin and Design

A simple Google search for images of *"Communist Manifesto"* reveals cover art containing symbols and signs with which we have become all too familiar. In fact, the symbols permeate modern society—the *hammer and sickle*, the *raised fist*, a *red star*, and various depictions of famous communist leaders such as Marx, Engels, Lenin, Stalin, and Mao.

Whichever version or translation of Marx's and Engels' book one has, the following summary presents accurately the predominant themes and overarching narrative of their classic work *The Communist Manifesto*. Their writings reveal the ideological framework underlying various historical movements which claim it to justify the means they employ in pursuit of revolution. The historical-contextual tie between Marx and Weishaupt is important because to understand those who influenced Marx is to facilitate a better interpretation of Marx's writings.

The Manifesto is the public declaration of social and political aims long held secret. In his introduction to the *Manifesto*, immediately before Section One, Marx says, "It is *high time* that communists should openly, in the face of the whole world, publish their views, their aims."[129] That it is "high time" to do anything implies that it should have been done long ago, and is suggestive of the fact that these "views" and "aims" have long been confined to secret councils.

Further, *The Manifesto* is intended to be a call to action. In it, Marx and Engels define the revolutionary tasks of a militant subset of the population in accordance with the particular circumstances within a given country. Vladimir Lenin, who put Marx's brutal ideology into practice and whose Bolsheviks won the Russian Revolution in 1917, helps today's misinformed American reader understand Marx's aims: "What Marx and Engels most of all criticize in...American Socialism" is that "they have reduced Marxism to a dogma, to a 'rigid (*starre*) orthodoxy,' that they consider it 'a *credo* and not a *guide* to action.'"[130] What's more, the danger of Marxist ideology is exacerbated because of its apparent fungibility. Hitler, for example, read Marx in 1913, and although he detested Marxist socialism, his *national socialism* substituted racial classes for economic classes in its ideology of a dialectical struggle toward utopia.[131]

The Manifesto is not merely political or economic theory, however. The allure of *The Manifesto* is that it provides a narrative of human history and social intercourse that exploits divisions between people and channels the rage of individuals into collective hatred.[132] It culminates with the issuance of a call to revolution—first, a civil war within one's own country, followed by the exportation of that revolution abroad.

In Section One, Marx characterizes all of history as a class struggle between "freeman and slave, patrician and plebeian, lord and serf...in a word, oppressor and oppressed."[133] Marx's oppressor versus oppressed narrative is developed using the idea of a clash between the Bourgeoisie (the class of modern Capitalists, the oppressor) and the Proletariat (the class of modern wage-laborers, the oppressed). In an invidious display of low-resolution, broadbrush stereotyping, Marx's narrative presupposes the virtue and justness of the oppressed class, and the evil and unjustness of the oppressor—an ideological assertion that is genocidal in its potential.

Continuing in Section One, free markets are castigated as "unconscionable," because they exploit the weak and oppressed all while "veiled in religious and political illusions."[134] Workers are "slaves" to their employers, and their wages are too low and unfairly established by the rulers.[135] Marx decries Capitalism as an attack on all that is holy, making specific mention of religion and the nuclear family—not because Marx is overly concerned about preserving either, but because his aims and the emotional attachment of his reader to those institutions make it expedient.

Marx also employs specific rhetoric that, while in his 1848 writings is meant as a derogatory reference to the Bourgeoisie, might be easily applied in principle thereafter to any institution that is deemed unacceptable: he uses terms like *"patriarchal* master," and *"perfect hierarchy* of officers," and *"slaves of* the bourgeois class, and "hourly enslaved."[136] As the oppressed class grows in size and strength, Marx theorizes that they naturally "form combinations" against the oppressor class, and "here and there the contest breaks out into riots."[137]

To be clear, to criticize Marx's ideological framework should not be mistaken as a diminution of the awful circumstances in which many workers found themselves in early- and mid-nineteenth century Europe. Marx's narrative has appeal for precisely that reason—because it draws heavily upon the genuinely deplorable experiences of the contemporary working class. And if revolution is what he and Engels sought, there simply was no better narrative that could be used to exploit the raw emotions of the masses.

The first section of *The Manifesto* draws to a close with Marxist ideology asserting itself as a comprehensive theory of war and peace, concluding with revelations that further justify the need for violent revolution. The aspiring practitioner is reminded that the struggle in which society is engaged is a class struggle, and that *because* one class is evil, there will always be fighting. Therefore, to eliminate the evil oppressor class—by force if necessary—is to eliminate conflict and to free the world of domination and exploitation. The happy expectation, of course, is that the elimination of the oppressor class will enable the remaining virtuous victor to abandon class struggle forevermore. As that violent clash approaches with increasing certainty—when the writing is on the wall—Marx foresees that the privileged class, the oppressor, will fracture, and some will even join the oppressed revolutionaries because they hope to gain favor with those whom they perceive as holding the future in their hands. Section One states:

> Finally, in times *when the class struggle nears the decisive hour,* the *process of dissolution going on within the ruling class, in fact within the whole range of old society, assumes such a violent, glaring character, that a small section of the ruling class cuts itself adrift, and joins the revolutionary class, the class that holds the future in its hands.* Just as, therefore, at an earlier period, a section of the nobility went over to the bourgeoisie, so now a portion of the bourgeoisie goes over to the proletariat.[138] (Italics added)

Marx's characterization of history as an ongoing and repeating class struggle may be overly simplistic, but his prediction that privileged members within society will align with the cause of revolutionaries out of fear and mere necessity is recognizable even today. Those in power, whose ambition it is to remain in power above all else, will compromise their pretended values when the stakes are high. If by chance the oppressor becomes revolutionary, "they are so," according to Marx, "only in view of their impending transfer into" the oppressed class.[139] "They thus defend not their present, but their future interests, they desert their own standpoint."[140] They believe that the conflict Marx predicts, and which his ideology advocates, will begin right here at home. Marx says:

> Though not in substance, yet in form, the struggle of the [oppressed class] with the [oppressor class] *is at first a national struggle.* The [oppressed class] of each country must, of course, *first of all settle matters with its own [oppressor class].*
>
> In depicting the most general phases of the development of the [oppressed class], we traced the *more or less veiled civil war,* raging within existing society, up to the point where that war *breaks out into open revolution, and where the violent overthrow of the [oppressor class] lays the foundation for the sway of the [oppressed class]....*
>
> And here it becomes evident, that *the [oppressor class] is unfit any longer to be the ruling class in society, and to impose its conditions of existence upon society* as an overriding law. It is unfit to rule because it is incompetent to assure an existence to its slave within his slavery, because it cannot help letting him sink into such a state, that it has to feed him, instead of being fed by him. Society can no longer live under this [oppressor class], *in other words, [the oppressor class'] existence is no longer compatible with society....*

What the [oppressor class], therefore, produces, above all,
is its own grave-diggers.[141] (Italics added)*

As Lenin observed, Marx's voice in some of these passages is beginning to be as prescriptive as it is descriptive. The "more or less veiled civil war" Marx describes will rage within society until it suddenly breaks out into open revolution. The civil war is "veiled" because its reality remains elusive to most people. It is a state of domestic social and political hostility that stops short of open warfare; that is, it might rightly be termed a cold civil war.[142] Marx predicts that when the revolution begins, those labeled as the oppressors will be violently overthrown. Once the victory is won at home, then the revolution can be exported internationally. This is the plan.

But will all the proletariat, or oppressed class, participate in the revolution? Not likely. For one thing, many do not believe they are oppressed, or that violence will somehow forge a path to a better life. Therefore, there is need of "other classes" to join in the fray. Those other classes are characterized by Marx in the following manner at the end of Section One:

> The 'dangerous class,' the social scum, that passively rotting mass thrown off by the lowest layers of old society, *may, here and there, be swept into the movement* by a proletarian revolution; its conditions of life, however, prepare it far more for the part of *a bribed tool of reactionary intrigue.*[143]

---

* In these passages, "bourgeoisie" and "proletariat" have been replaced with "oppressor class" and "oppressed class" respectively. This has been done to facilitate readability for those less familiar with the antiquated terms, and to make clear the ideology's transferability, or what I previously refered to as fungibility, depending on how a practitioner wants to define these classes (i.e. classes based on race rather than on economic stratification, such as Hitler did).

In Section Two, once Marx has laid a foundation built upon descriptions of history as characterized by class struggle, he proceeds to outline the aims of communism. Remember, he and Engels are addressing an international audience, as they intend their work to be published in the English, French, German, Italian, Flemish, and Danish languages.[144] He explains that the "immediate aim of the communists is the same as that of all the other proletarian parties: formation of the proletariat into a class, overthrow of the bourgeois supremacy, conquest of political power by the proletariat."[145] An essential feature in the accomplishment of those aims is the destruction of private property; not just any property, however, "but the abolition of bourgeois property," or the property of the oppressor.[146] Marx addresses—and abruptly dismisses—the critique that private property is "the ground work of all personal freedom, activity and independence"—a very American view, a country which sits atop the apex of bourgeois privilege.[147] We then get a rich taste of Marxist ideology when Marx compares communism with capitalism. Section Two states:

> In bourgeois society...*the past dominates the present*: *in Communist society, the present dominates the past*. In bourgeois society capital is independent and has individuality, while the living person is dependent and has no individuality.
>
> And the abolition of this state of things is called by the bourgeois, abolition of individuality and freedom! *And rightly so. The abolition of bourgeois individuality, bourgeois independence, and bourgeois freedom is undoubtedly aimed at....*
>
> In one word, you reproach us with intending to do away with your property. Precisely so; that is just what we intend.[148] (Italics added)

The idea that the past dominates the present in capitalist societies while the present dominates the past in communist societies is a false dichotomy, and yet there is no doubt that there is a true aspirational motive revealed in his assertion. Embedded within Marx's claim is manifest the ideological justification upon which totalitarian regimes, movements, and strongmen rely for the destruction of relics, symbols, and writings of the past. It justifies the destruction of *what is*, asserting that the revolution will bring about something that *will be* better. If the Capitalists are trying to control the people by having them look to the past, so the argument goes, then the past ought to be destroyed; traditional religious and cultural sites must come down, because they are, after all, only a symbol of the oppressor, those with privilege. They are vain monuments to those who unjustly wield power in old society. To maintain the vestiges of old society is to perpetuate oppression.

Marx and Engels understood that this ideologically justifiable destruction of *things* quickly becomes anger toward and resentment of *people*, particularly of those people who oppose the revolution's aims. Engels wrote: "A revolution is certainly the most authoritarian thing there is; it is the act whereby one part of the population *imposes its will upon* the other part by means of rifles, bayonets and cannon—*authoritarian means, if such there be at all*."[149] (Italics added) And lest we are duped into the utopian deception that once the oppressed class subdues the oppressor class, social and political conflict will cease, Engels adds: "And if the victorious party does not want to have fought in vain, *it must maintain this rule by means of the terror which its arms inspire*."[150] (Italics added) According to Marxist ideology, the peace of the administrative state comes later, just not yet.

For the remainder of Section Two, Marx addresses various criticisms that have been leveled against the communists. In addition to those criticisms mentioned above, they further include: Communism's attack on "individuality," its attack on "freedom, culture, and laws," its aim to abolish the nuclear family, its drive to establish socialized education, removing that responsibility from parents, and its "desiring to abolish countries and nationalism."[151]

Marx does not deny any of these criticisms but justifies them. It is not individuality *per se* that communists attack, only "bourgeois individuality," for those are the only individuals that matter in capitalist society. Marx insists: "This person," the bourgeois individual, must be *"swept out of the way, and made impossible."*[152]

It is not freedom, culture, and law writ large that the communists seek to abolish, only that freedom, culture, and law which is the product of bourgeois rule—it is to be dismantled and remade in favor of the new ruling class.

With regards to the family, Marx says that because of "capital" and "private gain," family only really exists among the bourgeois, and that once their capital is taken from them, their family relations will "vanish as a matter of course."[153]

With regards to children and wives, these are merely exploited by the bourgeois for purposes of production; all their "clap-trap about the family and education, about the hallowed co-relation of parent and child, becomes all the more disgusting" when considered in the light of modern industry, Marx explains. The oppressor class is responsible for the families of the oppressed class being "torn asunder."[154]

Last, with regards to religious objections to communism's aims, Marx simply explains they "are not deserving of serious examination."[155]

In light of all of that, and because it will be the main focus later in the last chapter, we briefly note here, once again, that the ideological assertion that a group of people must be "swept out of the way" and "made impossible," is rhetoric that portends genocide.

In Section Three of *The Manifesto*, Marx and Engels explore the various manifestations of socialism throughout Europe. While, in their view, some have merit, they are also critical of each of them. "The French socialist and communist literature" in particular was "emasculated," they note, because it did not adequately "express the struggle of one class with the other."[156] Instead of expressing the "interests of the proletariat," they chide, the literature defended "the interests of Human Nature, of Man in general, *who belongs to no class, has no reality, who exists only in the misty realm of philosophical fantasy.*"[157] (Italics added) This wrongheaded literature, they explain, "went to the extreme length of directly opposing the 'brutally destructive' tendency of communism, and of proclaiming its supreme and impartial contempt of all class struggles. With very few exceptions, all the so-called socialist and communist publications that now (1847) circulate in Germany belong to the domain of this foul and enervating literature." Thus, to the Marxist, Section Three firmly establishes the ideological roots that an individual's value is not inherent, but rather is determined by the class or group to which he or she belongs.

In the last section of *The Manifesto*, Section Four, the question "What is the position of the communists in relation to the various existing opposition parties throughout Europe?" is posited.

Its answer is revealing.

"In France," Marx and Engels explain, communists support "the Social-Democrats" who are fighting against the conservatives and bourgeoisie; "In Switzerland they support the Radicals;" "In Poland," communists support the party that "insists on an agrarian revolution," and which was the same party that fomented the insurrection of Cracow in 1846; "In Germany," communists temporarily support the "bourgeoisie whenever it acts in a revolutionary way," because it is hoped they will soon overthrow the monarchy—that once that revolution is accomplished, communists would turn their support to the Proletariat whom they expect will weaponize the "social and political conditions" to fight the new oppressor. They conclude:

In short, the *communists everywhere support every revolutionary movement against the existing social and political order* of things.

The communists disdain to conceal their views and aims. *They openly declare that their ends can be attained only by the forcible overthrow of all existing social conditions.* Let the ruling classes tremble....

WORKING MEN OF ALL COUNTRIES, UNITE![158] (Italics added)

That throughout history different groups of people, at different times and places, have been privileged above, or *in different ways than*, other groups of people, is true enough. However, the grounds for those class divisions, caste systems, hierarchical structures, power distributions, and social and cultural preferences and norms are more nuanced and complex than Marx indicates.

Let us here, then, assert why it is important to trace through the Manifesto in the kind of detail that we have. It is not simply to take issue with Marx's narrative of history. For, to be mistaken in one's grand theory of "the history of all hitherto existing society" is one thing. Rather, the issue is this: the ideological insistence that *because* one group of people is privileged it is *necessarily* a class of oppressors, and is *therefore* evil, all-too-naturally becomes justification for violence against that group.

Such a twisted view of humanity allows the practitioners of Marxism to harbor a victim mentality, and to point the finger at other citizens and blame them for life's difficulties. It breeds a fearful mentality that insists others are out to get them—the wealthy, the police, institutions of higher learning, religious groups, or certain races.

CHAPTER 5

MARXISM'S MANY FACES

The beginning of wisdom is to call things by their proper name.
Confucius

MUCH OF ONE'S TIME *in uniform is spent training. In my case, several of the past twenty-one years have been exclusively focused on it. Some of the many training courses I have completed include the Air Force Academy's two-part Basic Cadet Training (BCT, or "Beast") course, the Academy's summer Combat Survival Training (CST) course, its glider training program, Undergraduate Pilot Training (UPT), the Pilot Instructor Training (PIT) course, the Introduction to Fighter Fundamentals (IFF) course, the Air Force's Survival, Evasion, Resistance, and Escape (SERE) training program, a water survival training course, the F-15C Basic course, the F-15C Mission Qualification Training (MQT) course, the Undergraduate Space Training (UST) course, the Space-based Infrared System (SBIRS) Mission Qualification Training (MQT) course, the Space Operations Center (SOC) Commander training course, and a squadron commander training course. In addition to these training courses there have been many others—some merely hours long, while others spanned days or weeks. These trainings literally amount to years of my total time in uniform. Naturally, once "certified" in any major weapon system, what follows is more training.*

Excellence and competence are demanded of the military professional. That is as it should be—considering the nature of the profession, the American people wouldn't have it any other way. Many servicemembers are expected to become skilled warfighters, and those in uniform who support the warfighter similarly shoulder the burden of developing expertise in their own field. There is a direct correlation between the criticality and difficulty of any mission or weapon system and the difficulty, duration, and quality of the training program for that mission. For that reason, it takes years to correctly train and develop a talented fighter pilot, for example. For the same reason, not all training is created equal.

Though much of the training I've received in the Air and Space Forces has been worthwhile, one of my favorite training courses was the Air Force's SERE training program. Aircrew and special operations personnel are required to pass the three-week course in order to remain in their career fields, as their missions put them at the greatest risk of enemy capture. Like any of the best training programs offered by the Defense Department, the SERE school instructors and specialists are top-notch. And the training is difficult for good reason. Ideally, completion of the training program better equips servicemembers to "return with honor" should they ever have the misfortune of being held captive as a prisoner of war (POW) by a foreign enemy.

I was trained at the SERE school located at Fairchild Air Force Base in Washington State. After only several days of academics, trainees were bussed out to a remote location somewhere in the mountains—somewhere that seemed to me very north and very cold. When we arrived at our drop-off location, we all piled out of the bus burdened with gear and began our trek into the woods.

There were probably two feet of snow on the ground when we arrived. The ground, the trees, and the sky were all a brilliant white. The setting was serene, the woods beautiful. This was the beginning of the survival portion of our training—where you are taught both rudimentary as well as specialty survival skills—and it occurred during Thanksgiving, which added a kind of emotional and psychological sting on top of the hunger and cold since most of us would rather have been spending that time with family and friends.

To my surprise, it was not the snow or the freezing temperatures that gave us the most trouble. Snow, after all, was good for some things—water being just one. And the freezing temps kept that snow dry. It was actually when the temperatures rose above freezing and the precipitation turned to rain that we really became cold and survival became painful. Making fires at that point was improbable. Keeping clothes dry impossible. Yet even the rain had its advantages. Once we transitioned from the survival to the evasion phase of our training, our small teams were able to move about in the woods without detection as the sound of our footsteps disappeared with the noise of the rain.

As the name of the school implies, I was also trained in resistance techniques. Though I cannot disclose the specifics of the training, I can say that such training is meant to prepare those who might be captured for the emotional, physical, and psychological stress, abuse, torture, interrogation, indoctrination, and exploitation efforts they will likely encounter as a hostage or POW. It is emotionally, physically, and psychologically stressful training, and necessarily so. It is excellent training. It teaches you something about your own capacity for resilience in the face of terrible adversity. It trains you how to resist divulging sensitive information when it matters most.

My own training turns my thoughts to the many heroic men and women who have had to resist real captors' abusive exploitation efforts. I have read some of their stories. For example, I have always admired General Robbie Risner's memoir The Passing of the Night, wherein he describes the deprivation he and others endured as POWs in Vietnam. And there are many other courageous captives whose stories I've never heard—whose stories none of us have heard.

Before Vietnam, during the Korean War, hundreds of US Air Force men were held captive by Chinese communists in North Korea and China. After the Korean Armistice, 235 such men were returned by the Chinese to the United States. Not surprisingly, the US Air Force expended considerable effort to investigate the experiences of these men so that we might *have a full and accurate account of the tactics and techniques employed by these communist captors.*

On November 13, 1956, three years after the war ended, a report was presented at a combined meeting of the Section on Neurology and Psychiatry at The New York Academy of Medicine as part of a panel discussion on "Communist Methods of Interrogation and Indoctrination." The report focuses primarily on Chinese communist efforts to extort "false confessions" from American prisoners, something half of American POWS experienced while in captivity. Rather than inflict physical violence, as the prisoners perhaps feared most, the communist captors would seek to manipulate the beliefs, statements, and conduct of prisoners by establishing controlled environments and through the extortion of false confessions.[159]

Why coerce false confessions?

Because, at least for some prisoners, the repetition of false confessions of guilt over time convinced them they were actually guilty. Acquiescence to the idea of one's own actual guilt, in turn, bred self-loathing, self-resentment, generated an internal struggle that was more successful than even the exogenously imposed torment of a captor. In the end, it was psychologically crippling, turning the captive into a compliant pawn.

As it turns out, Americans were rather resilient at first, however, and slow to comply with the demands of their captors. But the Chinese captors were patient, and they considered time to be on their side. In weighing a pile of testimony and evidence, American scientists and psychologists came to believe that the communist captors were mostly interested in forced confessions as a type of "teaching procedure." They were teaching, or training, as noted above, American POWS to be compliant, to build a habit of "confessor behavior," and for apparently no other reason than for the sake of compliance itself. "Shaping" human compliance was an end worth pursuing even if it was a slow process.[160] Scientists further found that the methods used by the Chinese communists were not uniquely their own but had been used for decades wherever communist regimes had been established.[161]

The Geneva Conventions of August 12, 1949, which, among other things, establish the standards of international law for the humanitarian treatment of combatants during war, expressly prohibit any form of "coercion" used "to secure from [POWS] information of any kind whatever."[162] *Perhaps you think that's unlikely, and you'd probably be right, but just wait till you read the next sentence—the language in Part III, Section I, Article 17 goes so far as to say that POWs who "refuse to answer" the questions put to them by their captors "may not be threatened, insulted, or exposed to any unpleasant or disadvantageous treatment of any kind."*[163]

Did you catch that? According to international law, even prisoners are not to be threatened. Even prisoners are not to be insulted or exposed to any unpleasant treatment of any kind. That's what the law says.

What I find incredibly ironic is that as a country, at present, we come nowhere close to holding ourselves to a similar standard of conduct toward even our own citizens. We abuse one another in ways prohibited by international law as unlawful for the treatment of prisoners held during war. Systemically, this is true.

Do partisan hacks and progressive Leftist ideologues refrain from using threats, insults, and unpleasant or disadvantageous treatment of American citizens who choose to believe, think, speak, and act in ways that do not conform to their own standards? No, they do not.

Why is it that there is an entire industry in the United States that is paid to employ these same coercive and manipulative tactics against the American people? Why are taxpayers funding this industry so that federal employees—men and women in uniform even—can be incessantly exposed to threats, insults, and unpleasant and disadvantageous treatment if they refuse to acknowledge and confess their guilt? Their privilege?

I am talking about the Diversity, Equity, and Inclusion industry. The industry appears to be seeking to actively "shape compliance" of our men and women in uniform—ensuring patterns of "confessor behavior" are established for our young military servicemembers.

Why do we allow this?

Why doesn't somebody—anybody—in the senior leadership circles of our military stand up against it? Perhaps they have tried but have been unsuccessful. Perhaps they are unaware, or naïve.

How is it that we have become so compliant so quickly?

I agree with former law and political science professor Carol Swain who recently said that the Diversity, Equity, and Inclusion industry is among the greatest threats facing American society.[164]

That is true because the industry is steeped in critical race theory.

Critical race theory is dangerous and divisive because it is rooted in Marxist ideology.

Postmodernism and Political Correctness

LEARNING THE BASIC CONCEPTS of Marxist ideology helps one understand *the what* behind the current identity-based group struggles appearing in the United States. It is to get a look at the underlying ideological foundation for alternative narratives about American history, such as those "reframings" of American history undertaken by the likes of Howard Zinn and Nikole Hannah-Jones, discussed in Chapter 1.

In Chapters 3 and 4, we took a closer look at *the what* that is Marxism. The things discussed in the remainder of the book have their roots in that ideology. In a way, everything that follows hereafter is either a direct outgrowth of Marxist thought or has been somehow influenced and shaped by the ideology and its adherents.

But understanding *the what* still leaves one asking about *the how* and *the why*. *How is it,* for example, that American people and institutions—predominantly our education system, and now, all federal agencies including even our military services—increasingly resonate and align with Marxist ideology? (If there remains any question in your mind that we do, then the next several chapters may help flip the light switch for you.)

How is it that Americans can now so easily question and forget the greatness of the American ideal and succumb to the communist tactics of subversion described above?

How did we get to the point as a country where we have cozied up to Marxism, and *why* can we not recognize our now-rapid slide into various Marxist schools of thought and forms of activism for what it is?

How and why are these things happening?

"Two ways," to borrow Hemmingway's clever phrase, "Gradually, then suddenly."[165]

Finding answers to these questions can be difficult because the simplest answers are often hard to stomach, and the nuanced and complex answers harder to conceptualize and accurately articulate. Some authors have already done an excellent job in the latter arena. But diving headlong into their richly thought-provoking works is beyond my interests for what I hope this book will accomplish.

Three books that come first to mind, however, that are a great start into answering *the how* and *the why* include Helen Pluckrose's and James Lindsay's new book *Cynical Theories: How Activist Scholarship Made Everything about Race, Gender, and Identity—and Why This Harms Everybody*; Stephen Hicks' book *Explaining Postmodernism: Skepticism and Socialism from Rousseau to Foucault;* and Douglass Murray's *Madness of Crowds: Gender, Race, and Identity.* These books are included in the suggested reading list at the end of this book.

Briefly, we consider the following. Pluckrose and Lindsay describe how the kind of authoritarian changes rapidly occurring in our institutions at once become difficult to understand because they "stem from a very peculiar view of the world—one that even speaks its own language, in a way." In *Cynical Theories* they explain how the progressive Left has aligned itself "not with Modernity but with postmodernism, which rejects objective truth as a fantasy."[166] Describing postmodernist Social Justice activists, they continue:

> Within the English-speaking world, they speak English, but they use everyday words differently from the rest of us. When they speak of "racism," for example, *they are*

not referring to prejudice on the grounds of race, but rather to, as they define it, a racialized system that permeates all interactions in society yet is largely invisible except to those who experience it or who have been trained in the proper "critical" methods that train them to see it. (These are the people sometimes referred to as being "woke," meaning awakened, to it.) This very precise technical usage of the word inevitably bewilders people, and, in their confusion, they may go along with things they wouldn't if they had a common frame of reference to help them understand what is actually meant by the word.[167]

Postmodernism is a radical worldview—a radically skeptical and cynical one—and you and I are living in a postmodern world. This is true despite the fact that most Americans do not accept its philosophical premises. The philosophy of postmodernism was developed by French theorists who revolutionized social philosophy by launching an assault on reason.[168] In their writings, you will find references to earlier philosophers such as Immanuel Kant, Georg W.F. Hegel, and Karl Marx. French philosopher Jacques Derrida (1930-2004), the founder of "deconstruction" and a leader of the postmodernists, described his own ideas as a radicalized form of Marxism—a frightening admission when made in the face of the global rubble left behind in the aftermath of the twentieth century's communist revolutions.[169]

Postmodernism really took off during the 1960s, though its philosophical foundations were laid in relatively obscure corners of academia in the decades preceding the 60s. Since then, postmodern thought has crept out into the rest of society, has overtaken the public education system, and is the driving impulse behind illiberal ideological movements pursuing the broad goal called "Social Justice."[170] The Social Justice Movement—not to be confused with legitimate social justice, which is a good thing—imposes new speech codes upon society and coerces compliance by imposing devastating consequences for the non-woke citizen's career and reputation.[171]

Postmodern thought deliberately attacks science and reason in an effort to reshape society. It asserts that individuals possess no independent meaning—that only one's group identity or affiliation gives them meaning. Similar to Marxism, it divides society into "dominant and marginalized identities," asserting that society is itself underpinned by "invisible systems of white supremacy, patriarchy, heteronormativity, cisnormativity, ableism, and fatphobia.[172] Again, from *Cynical Theories*:

> We find ourselves faced with the continuing disman-tlement of categories like knowledge and belief, reason and emotion, and men and women, and with increasing pressures to censor our language in accordance with The Truth According to Social Justice. We see *radical relativism in the form of double standards, such as assertions that only men can be sexist and only white people can be racist,* and in the wholesale rejection of consistent principles of nondiscrimination. In the face of this, it grows increas-ingly difficult and even dangerous to argue that people should be treated as individuals or to urge recognition of our shared humanity in the face of divisive and con-straining identity politics.[173]

Postmodernism challenges the possibility of obtaining objective knowledge of the world—of knowing truth. Reason and truth are meaningless; they are merely abstractions. Objectivity is a myth. It follows, therefore, that all interpretations of the world are equally valid, according to postmodernists. Fortunately for the rest of us, despite their claim that all interpretations of the world are equally valid, their own *disproportionate criticisms of* certain interpretations of the world—namely, traditional Western interpretations of the world—betray their motives. Not coincidentally, postmodernists are leftist in their politics—in many cases, far left.

The philosophical construction of postmodernism was necessary, in part, because of widespread "disillusionment with Marxism," and, according to Pluckrose and Lindsay, "the waning credibility of religious worldviews."[174] Such disillusionment did not mean that Marxism vanished, though. It was simply transformed. Its transformation gave it new names—lots of them—and new masks to wear. While the founders of postmodernism dabbled in the realms of surrealist art and antirealist philosophy, their bread and butter became the arena of revolutionary politics.[175] As Jordan Peterson explains of the postmodernist movement, through the employment of a "linguistic sleight-of-hand," barely repentant Marxists who inhabited the intellectual pinnacles of the West were provided the "means to retain their [Marxist] world-view" in postmodernism.[176]

There are many other schools of thought, or theories, that are interconnected with and, in some ways, dependent upon post-modernism and, therefore, share its Marxist roots. Some of them perhaps sound familiar to you: "political correctness," "feminism and gender studies," "black studies," "queer theory," "postcolonial theory," "intersectionality," "Social Justice" scholarship and activism, "identity politics," and "critical theory" and its variants. It is the last of these, *critical theory* (CT), including its most recent outgrowth, *critical race theory* (CRT), to which we turn our attention for the remainder of this chapter.

Remember, one thing postmodernism cannot do is put forth a true worldview—after all, there is no such thing as objective truth and therefore no true worldview. As with postmodernism, CT and CRT likewise have no objective truths to offer. Instead, they offer only criticisms of and accusations about others.

At best, critical race theory has poisonous effects upon the culture of free speech. At worst, it becomes a tool in the hands of authoritarian bullies—one more way in which Marxists can extort false confessions of guilt and shape human compliance.

The New Intolerance*

Critical race theory makes race the prism through which its proponents analyze all aspects of American life. It provides a substitute narrative to compete with the traditional American philosophical and historical narrative that has shaped our culture and values. It establishes a new foundation for the continued promulgation of identity politics in America. By it, the Marxist hopes to facilitate the achievement of violent revolution, while the compassionate but ignorant "tool of reactionary intrigue" simply hopes to remake American society into something she has been trained to believe is more just and equitable.

As its name makes clear, *critical race theory* is a mutation of *critical theory*, which had its beginning in a 1937 manifesto of the Frankfurt School. The Frankfurt School, based on Moscow's Marx-Engels Institute, was originally going to be named the *Institut fur Marxismus* (Institute for Marxism), but its founders decided to adopt the less provocative Institute for Social Research in Frankfurt. From the beginning, CT was an unremitting attack on Western institutions and norms in order to tear them down. Its proponents became chiefly concerned with revealing "hidden biases and underexamined assumptions."[177]

Even though the Frankfurt School's manifesto was issued during the height of Stalin's deadly holocaust in the Soviet Union, the school itself maintained almost complete official silence about those events. The school's second director and author of the manifesto, Max Horkheimer, claimed that "traditional theory fetishized knowledge, seeing truth as empirical and universal. Critical Theory, on the other hand, 'held that man could not be objective and that there are no universal truths.'"[178]

---

*The name of this section and much of the section's content are taken from recent work done by The Heritage Foundation in a superb Backgrounder called "Critical Race Theory, the New Intolerance, and Its Grip on America," written by Jonathan Butcher and Mike Gonzales and published December 7, 2020. I recommend reading their work in its entirety. It can be found here: http://report.heritage.org/bg3567.

Not surprisingly, there is a bitter karma in store for those who wittingly adopt such a foolish notion. Sooner or later, they lose touch with objective reality; the ideological paradigm they adopt infects their capacity for right reason, and the light of their conscience fades—everything bends toward the relative and away from the objective. Soon, there is nothing left but radical relativism.

The relativism of critical theory has its ideological roots in Friedrich Nietzsche and has been filtered and re-sculptured based upon the ideas of Hegel and Marx. Horkheimer made clear his views on Marxism and the communist state in his collection of short essays known as the *Dammerung* (in German, both "dawn" and "twilight"). He wrote: "He who has eyes for the meaningless injustice of the imperialist world…will regard the events in Russia [a reference to the Bolshevik Revolution] as the *progressive*, painful attempt to overcome this injustice."[179] (Italics added) Horkheimer's and the Frankfurt School's ideas were a resurfacing of the ideas that nearly a century earlier gained prominence by the pens of Marx and Engels, and a half-century before that, in the secret meetings of Adam Weishaupt.

The communist revolutions of the working class predicted by Marx and Engels never did take hold in the West as many communists had hoped. After publishing *The Communist Manifesto* in 1848, Marx and Engels spent decades writing thousands of letters to comrades around the world, including those in America and throughout the West, in hopes of helping others capture a glimpse of the international revolutionary vision they held. Following the successful revolution of the Russian Bolsheviks in 1917, which was the first successful Marxist revolution in history that resulted in the establishment of a communist state, communist parties sprang up across the globe. Communist Party USA (CPUSA) was formed in 1919, by which time dozens of communist parties were forming in other countries. Still, by the early 1930s, there seemed to be little hope of a revolution in

America, and the official CPUSA membership numbers remained below 20,000.

In that context, critical theory's demolition of Western traditions and norms emerged as a tool to implement the "counter-hegemony" called for in the *Theory of Cultural Hegemony* enunciated by Italian philosopher Antonio Gramsci (1891-1937), the founder of the Italian Communist party. The idea of Gramsci's counter-hegemony strategy, according to neo-Gramscian theorist Nicola Pratt, is one of dismantling the incumbent hegemon by creating an "alternative hegemony on the terrain of civil society in preparation for political change."[180] Gramsci himself had come to believe that the reason the working class was not revolting and overthrowing the bourgeoisie was *because they were culturally aligned with the ruling class*. America's thriving civil society thus posed a tough case for the Marxist revolutionary. American *culture*, therefore, became the object of the Marxist assault.

Jonathan Butcher and Mike Gonzalez, in their Heritage Foundation Backgrounder titled "Critical Race Theory, the New Intolerance, and its Grip on America," write:

> Gramsci had come to believe that the workers were not revolting and overthrowing the bourgeoisie *because they had bought into the belief system* of the ruling class—family, nation-state, the capitalist system, and God. What was needed was *struggle sessions in which the revolutionary vanguard would teach the workers how to think*. But *first the norms needed to be torn down*. That is where Critical Theory—and, as we will see, all its offshoots—come in.[181] (Italics added)

Horkheimer and his Marxist cohort from the Frankfurt School would end up fleeing Germany to escape the Third Reich, importing critical theory first to Geneva, then to New York. There, Columbia University allowed them to organize themselves in

1935 at Teacher's College. Coincident with their arrival, the membership numbers of CPUSA grew rapidly, more than tripling by the end of the decade.[182] These scholars quickly developed a disdain for the American worker because of his reluctance to depart from American culture. "They insist unwaveringly on the ideology by which they are enslaved," Horkheimer wrote of the American worker.[183]

After the defeat of the Nazi regime, Horkheimer and others of his colleagues returned to Germany. Horkheimer's assistant, Herbert Marcuse (1898-1979) stayed behind to become one of the leading spokesmen for the New Left.

While Marcuse and Marx pursued similar aims, each adopted a somewhat different approach for the accomplishment of those aims. For example, in mid-nineteenth century Europe, as we saw in Chapter 4, Marx believed the working class was the most likely pool of candidates to rise up and accomplish the overthrow of the existing power structure. To that end, he and Engels built their oppressor versus oppressed narrative centering on the proletariat and bourgeoisie.

As for Marcuse, after witnessing upheavals in the 1960s and 1970s caused by the riots and violence associated with the Civil Rights era and the anti-Vietnam War movement, he came to realize Marx's traditional oppressed working-class narrative was not the ripest agent of social and political change. Rather, in mid-twentieth century America, it was minorities that could be used as the new agents of change. "Underneath the conservative popular base is the substratum of the outcasts and outsiders, the exploited and persecuted of other races and other colors," Marcuse wrote. And he recognized that even though there existed great revolutionary potential among these minorities, they would still *need to be led ideologically*—"their opposition is revolutionary even if their consciousness is not."[184]

Marcuse's sense was correct. In America, race-based narratives work well at creating revolutionary fervor. According to former black communist activist Manning Johnson, Marxists in the United States had already been exploiting justifiable and seeming grievances for decades in order to "transform idealism into a cold and ruthless weapon against the capitalist system."[185] Johnson had been inducted into the Communist Party in the 1930s largely because of the preaching of a communist Bishop in the Episcopal Church, William Montgomery Brown, and was one of many African Americans who were being used by the communists to ignite revolution. After laboring in the cause of communism ten years, Johnson left the movement, became a witness against subversives before the House Un-American Activities Committee (HUAC), and later wrote a book titled *Color, Communism, & Common Sense* (1958), hoping that he could open others' eyes to the traps to which he himself had fallen prey.

The communist ideology and tactics Johnson recounts in his short book are striking because of their similarities with what American's saw daily in the news in 2020. He recalls receiving "two years of practical training in organizing street demonstrations, inciting mob violence, how to fight the police and how to politically 'throw a brick and hide.'"[186] He explains that CPUSA, which functioned under the direction of the USSR's Politburo, was trying to build politically progressive groups in organizations such as the National Association for the Advancement of Colored People (NAACP), and other youth, religious, fraternal, and labor organizations.[187] These groups were not necessarily even comprised solely of those who understood and believed in communism's aims, but also of "fellow-travelers, sympathizers, liberals, etc."[188] These willing and unwitting participants constituted the vehicle on which Marxist revolutionaries pinned their hopes of victory. "Stirring up race and class conflict" was the basis of all discussion of CPUSA's work in the South, according to Johnson.[189] "The evil genius, Stalin, and the other megalomaniacal leaders in Moscow ordered the use of all racial, economic and social differences, no matter how small or insignificant, to start local fires of discontent, conflict and revolt....Black rebellion was what Moscow wanted. Bloody racial conflict would split America."[190]

Critical Legal Theory

Critical legal theory (CLT) became the first major offshoot of critical theory. Naturally, it emerged and blossomed within academia. Scholars of CLT readily acknowledge the direct influences of Marxism and postmodernism. From the Cornell Law School's Legal Information Institute: "Although CLS [Critical Legal Studies] has been largely contained within the United States, it was influenced to a great extent by European philosophers, such as Karl Marx, Max Weber, Max Horkheimer, Antonio Gramsci, and Michel Foucault."[191] From the same page, we read:

> Critical legal studies (CLS) is a theory which states that the law is necessarily intertwined with social issues, particularly stating that *the law has inherent social biases.* Proponents of CLS believe that *the law supports the interests of those who create the law.* As such, CLS states that the law supports *a power dynamic which favors the historically privileged* and disadvantages the historically underprivileged. CLS finds that the wealthy and the powerful use *the law as an instrument for oppression* in order to maintain their place in hierarchy. *Many in the CLS movement want to overturn the hierarchical structures of modern society and they focus on the law as a tool in achieving this goal.*[192] (Italics added)

Butcher and Gonzalez observe that "just as with Critical Theory, Critical Legal Theory is, then, an instrument to overturn society for those who follow its tenets, this time from a legal perspective." They continue:

The law, [critical legal scholars] argue, *is simply the cultural hegemony* codified in statutes and defended by a jurisprudence that aims to support the powerful against the claims of the marginalized. CLT proponents trace their founding to the first Conference on Critical Legal Studies, held at the University of Wisconsin at Madison in 1977. Among its main theorists figure Duncan Kennedy, Roberto Mangabeira Unger, and Robert W. Gordon.

In a 2002 essay, Kennedy acknowledges the debt Critical Legal Theory owes to both Marxism and post-modernism (championed by a mostly Parisian set of intellectuals who preached that texts could be "deconstructed" by the reader, a complicated philosophical concept that involves *reinterpreting words to replace ideas* based on objective physical existence), two separate critiques of bourgeois reality that nevertheless can rub uneasily against each other. "Critical Legal Studies," he writes, "operates [sic] at the uneasy juncture of two distinct, sometimes complimentary and sometimes conflicting enterprises, which I will call the left and the modernist/post-modernist projects."

"Leftism aims to transform existing social structures on the basis of a critique of their injustice, and, *specifically, at the injustices of racist, capitalist patriarchy. The goal is to replace the system, piece by piece or in medium- or large-sized blocs, with a better system,*" writes Kennedy. Post-modernism is a much more complex phenomenon, but it aims at the same destruction of society as the Marxist project, starting with the use of reason itself.[193] (Italics added)

Critical legal theorists such as Kennedy believe that the incessant criticism of racial injustices will fuel the emergence of the very identity groups Marcuse predicted would be the new revolutionary base. Kennedy quotes approvingly his fellow university professor Cornell

West to assert the existence of an "inchoate, scattered yet gathering progressive movement that is emerging across the American landscape. This gathering *now lacks both the vital moral vocabulary and the focused leadership* that can constitute and sustain it. Yet it will be rooted ultimately in current activities *by people of color, by labor and ecological groups, by women, by homosexuals.*"[194] (Italics added)

Note once again the fact that there is a deliberate focus on language—"the vital moral vocabulary"—because critical theorists and postmodernists know that by manipulating the meaning of words it is possible to replace old ideas with new ones. The imposition of this sort of confusion of tongues upon society makes radical shifts not only possible but inevitable—at first, gradually and imperceptibly, and then suddenly. Tragically, in both cases, the unraveling traditional social structure is difficult to rescue. Consequently, an increasingly polarized population is rendered mutually incomprehensible.

Kennedy further comments on the direction the political Left was headed in America. He adds that "in the United States, by the end of the 1970s, with the rise of identity politics, *left discourse merged with liberal discourse*, and the two ideas of the rights of the oppressed and the constitutional validity of their legal claims superseded all earlier versions of rightness."[195] What Kennedy is saying is tough to untangle, but important to understand. Restated, this merger of *Marxism* (which Kennedy refers to here as "left discourse") with the *modern Left* (which Kennedy refers to as "liberal discourse") resulted in two competing rights philosophies being introduced into Leftist American political discourse. The result was tantamount to an internal fracture. And now, a dilemma had arisen.

Should the New Left honor America's traditional belief that every individual possesses certain inalienable rights?

Or should it honor the new competing (Marxist) belief that the rights of oppressed groups of people superseded "all earlier versions of rightness," thus granting government the justification—the obligation even—to impose upon individual liberties so as to ensure the rights of oppressed groups are met?

Over time, the extent to which the Left has settled upon the un-American philosophy of the rights of oppressed or disadvantaged groups—now so often used in furtherance of an anti-American agenda—is the extent to which it has become an afront to American values. This slide towards Marxist ideology made the Left a welcoming host of postmodernist critical thought.

Today, critical legal scholars at Harvard University help us make the link between CLT and the now-popular and pervasive *critical race theory*. The Harvard Berkman Klein Center's page on Critical Legal Theory says that CLT scholars:

> ...focused from the start on the ways that *law contributed to illegitimate social hierarchies*, producing domination of women by men, *nonwhites by whites*, and the poor by the wealthy. They claim that apparently neutral language and institutions, operated through law, *mask relationships of power* and control. The emphasis on individualism within the law similarly *hides patterns of power relationships* while making it more difficult to summon up a sense of community and human interconnection.[196]

Critical Race Theory

The jump from the narrative outlined by Harvard scholars to CRT is not a difficult one to make. Critical race theory essentially makes everything about race. The persistence with which its proponents use it as a tool to implement identity politics and thus destroy American society means that it now touches every aspect of American life.

Derrick Bell, the widely acknowledged "godfather" of CRT, helps us better understand the role of CRT authors. He says their work "is often disruptive because its *commitment to anti-racism* goes well beyond civil rights, integration, affirmative action, and other liberal measures."[197] (Italics added) To go "well beyond" these other liberal measures in an attempt to "disrupt" American society is to land oneself in the "hard" left, or what communist-turned-conservative intellectual David Horowitz referred to as the "neo-communist" camp.[198]

One such CRT author, Angela Harris, is quoted by Bell in his essay titled "Who's Afraid of Critical Race Theory?" to affirm CRT's ideological inheritance from its CLT ancestor. What ideological inheritance, one might ask? The drive to dismantle all aspects of society through unremitting criticism.

In the same essay, Bell also cites theorist and professor Charles Lawrence and says he "speaks for many critical race theory adherents when he disagrees with the notion that laws are or can be written from a neutral perspective." Because the law "systematically privileges subjects who are white," CRT calls for a "transformative resistance strategy."[199] Critical race theorists make no apology for the truth that CRT is a political weapon to be used to transform American society and culture.

In the minds of activists, because of its intended uses, CRT no longer belonged merely within the protected walls of the university, where it had been confined for far too long. It had undoubtedly accomplished its work there, but the resistance strategy necessitated implementation in the real world. In the words of Marx, it was "high time" the tool be used to actually transform society.

One of the ways this transformation might be accomplished, as noted earlier, was through the creation of a new vocabulary. In just one such example, critical race theorist Kimberly Crenshaw came up with the term "intersectionality," which enables woke victims to recognize they are oppressed in more ways than just one. By citing association with more than one social group, or "axis," victims can recognize that there are potentially numerous reasons for their oppression.

As explained by CRT writers Patricia Hill Collins and Sirma Bilge, with intersectionality, "people's lives and the organization of power in a given society are better understood as being shaped not by a single axis of social division, be it race or gender or class, but by many axes that work together to influence each other."[200] The result is that people are trained to look for power imbalances, bigotry, and biases that they assume must be present—even "unconscious" biases, which, by definition, are unrecognizable to the persons who possess them.[201] Everything is reduced to prejudice. Besides intersectionality, there are other new terms invoked by CRT adherents that we will encounter later in this chapter.

Of the three *critical* schools of thought we have mentioned, CRT is considered the most explicitly and purposely political. Yet, it is this particular school that has finally made its appearance within the military services like a dangerous and unanticipated flash flood. It uses story-telling—often fictionalized and sensationalized stories—in order to portray America as a systemically racist country that seeks to keep down people of color. Its ceaseless assault is not confined merely to American institutions, but is extended to America's founding philosophy, values, and cultural identity.

Of note, the radical nature of CRT's philosophy and approach pits its adherents against the original goals of the Civil Rights movement, which largely sought to redeem America's promise by calling for a color-blind equality—the kind of equality, by the way, that the military has led the way in for decades.

Diversity & Inclusion Trainings

What is perhaps most surprising about all of this is that what began in academia as anti-American rhetoric and ideology, propagated by Leftist intellectuals—Marxists—who hated America's exceptionalism and founding philosophy, and whose intention was the deliberate dismantling of our institutions and the restructuring of our culture, is now believed by some leaders within America's military. They are so bought-in, themselves, that it comes as a surprise to them when patriotic servicemembers are not enthusiastic about their views.

The late American scholar Hugh Nibley warned of the condition in which we now find ourselves: "When those who referee the game become the leading practitioners of deception, the civilization is finished. Nothing stops the corrosive progress of rhetoric once it begins to work, for the highest achievement of the art, the ancients tell us, is that skill which convinces the patron, customer, or victim that no rhetoric at all is being used."[202]

Perhaps the victory of Marx in our day, then, is that we as patrons are unaware of his aims, strategy, and tactics. Marxist ideology and rhetoric—narratives about oppressor and oppressed groups, unacceptable power structures, racial group identities, and unfair economic stratifications—have once again come knocking at the door and we have all but let down our guard. Some senior military leaders are becoming the leading practitioners of this deception, this grand fraud, which seeks to unravel the moral fabric of America that once knit us together in unity.

Under the banner of "Diversity and Inclusion" trainings, some leaders unethically use their positions to promote CRT's divisive agenda and anti-American propaganda to the military personnel at their bases. I mentioned one such example in the vignette at the beginning of Chapter 2. As a result, we are seeing increased division and resentment within the ranks. We are seeing good order and discipline undermined. We are eroding the confidence military professionals place in their oath to support and defend the Constitution of the United States.

Fortunately, every base is different, as is every leader. There is yet hope that once the broader military community becomes aware of what is happening, more courageous and patriotic servicemembers of all ranks—across the political spectrum—will take a stand against CRT's destructive impulse. It is one of the purposes for which I am writing this book.

During the summer and fall months of 2020, it came to the attention of the White House that Diversity and Inclusion trainings were steeped in critical race theory, and that the trainings were spreading throughout Executive Branch agencies. The Trump Administration took swift action to intervene.

On September 4, 2020, the Director of the Office of Management and Budget (OMB), Russ Vought, issued a memorandum (M-20-34) for "The Heads of Executive Departments and Agencies" with the subject "Training in the Federal Government" addressing the matter. In it, Vought explains:

> It has come to the President's attention that Executive Branch agencies have spent millions of taxpayer dollars to date "training" government workers to believe divisive, anti-American propaganda.
>
> For example...employees across the Executive Branch have been required to attend trainings where they are told that "virtually all White people contribute to racism" or where they are required to say that they "benefit from racism."...
>
> These types of "trainings" not only run counter to the fundamental beliefs for which our Nation has stood since its inception, but they also engender division and resentment within the Federal workforce....[W]e cannot accept our employees receiving training that seeks to undercut our core values as Americans and drive division within our workforce.
>
> The President has directed me to ensure that Federal agencies cease and desist from using taxpayer dollars to fund these divisive, un-American propaganda training sessions....[A]ll agencies are directed to begin to identify all contracts or other agency spending related to any training on "critical race theory," "white privilege," or any other training or propaganda effort that teaches or

suggests either (1) that the United States is an inherently evil or racist country or (2) that any race or ethnicity is inherently racist or evil....

The President, and his Administration, are fully committed to the fair and equal treatment of all individuals in the United States. The President...intends to continue to support all Americans, regardless of race, religion, or creed. The divisive, false, and demeaning propaganda of the critical race theory movement is contrary to all we stand for as Americans and should have no place in the Federal government.[203]

In light of the context of the material presented in this book until now, the wisdom and timeliness of the OMB memorandum should be clear to anyone with common sense who cares about the preservation of their country and liberty.

The memo was spot-on.

Government workers were (and are), in fact, being trained to believe divisive, anti-American propaganda. Military servicemembers were (and are), in fact, being told that virtually all white people contribute to racism or were told to say that they benefit from racism. And these types of trainings do, in fact, run counter to the fundamental beliefs for which our Nation has stood since its inception, and engender division and resentment within the Federal workforce.

President Trump therefore directed OMB to ensure Federal agencies "cease and desist" from using taxpayer dollars to fund these training sessions. The memorandum also promised forthcoming detailed guidance on implementing the President's direction.

Several weeks later, the OMB memorandum was followed by an executive order (EO 13950) from President Trump on September 22, 2020, titled "Executive Order on Combating Race and Sex Stereotyping."[204] Once again, like the OMB memorandum, the language was spot-on. Pertinent excerpts of that EO are included here:

From the battlefield of Gettysburg to the bus boycott in Montgomery and the Selma-to-Montgomery marches, heroic Americans have valiantly risked their lives to ensure that their children would grow up in a Nation living out its creed, expressed in the Declaration of Independence: "We hold these truths to be self-evident, that all men are created equal." It was this belief in the inherent equality of every individual that inspired the Founding generation to risk their lives, their fortunes, and their sacred honor to establish a new Nation, unique among the countries of the world. President Abraham Lincoln understood that this belief is "the electric cord" that "links the hearts of patriotic and liberty-loving" people, no matter their race or country of origin. It is the belief that inspired the heroic black soldiers of the 54th Massachusetts Infantry Regiment to defend that same Union at great cost in the Civil War. And it is what inspired Dr. Martin Luther King, Jr., to dream that his children would one day "not be judged by the color of their skin but by the content of their character."

Thanks to the courage and sacrifice of our forebears, America has made significant progress toward realization of our national creed, particularly in the 57 years since Dr. King shared his dream with the country.

Today, however, many people are pushing *a different vision of America that is grounded in hierarchies based on collective social and political identities rather than in the inherent and equal dignity of every person as an individual. This ideology is rooted in the pernicious and false belief that America is irredeemably racist and sexist country; and that racial and sexual identities are more important than our common status as human beings and Americans.*

This destructive ideology is grounded in misrepresentations of our country's history and its role in the world. Although presented as new and revolutionary, they resurrect the discredited notions of the nineteenth century's apologists for slavery who, like President Lincoln's rival Stephen A. Douglas, maintained that our government "was made on the white basis" "by white men, for the benefit of white men." *Our Founding documents reject these racialized views of America,* which were soundly defeated on the blood-stained battlefields of the Civil War. Yet they are now being repackaged and sold as cutting-edge insights. *They are designed to divide us* and to prevent us from uniting as one people in pursuit of one common destiny for our great country.

Unfortunately, this malign ideology is now migrating from the fringes of American society and threatens to infect core institutions of our country. Instructors and materials teaching that men and members of certain races, as well as our most venerable institutions, are inherently sexist and racist are *appearing in workplace diversity trainings across the country,* even in components of the Federal Government and among Federal contractors.[205] (Italics added)

The EO cites examples of inappropriate training materials from the Department of the Treasury, Argonne National Laboratories, Sandia National Laboratories, and the Smithsonian Institution. Direct quotations out of the training materials from these various agencies specifically state that "virtually all White people, regardless of how 'woke' they are, contribute to racism," and that racism is "interwoven into every fabric of America." "White males" are denigrated in the training materials and are criticized as placing an unhealthy emphasis on "rationality over emotionality." Some trainings, which were presented only to non-minority audiences, asked those present to "acknowledge" their "privilege" to each other. "All of this," the EO continues, "is contrary to the fundamental premises underpinning our Republic: *that all individuals are created equal and should be allowed an equal opportunity under the law to pursue happiness and prosper based on individual merit.*" (Italics added)

The "Uniformed Services" are specifically mentioned in EO 13950. The services are reminded they should continue to foster environments devoid of hostility grounded in race or sex, and that they must always be committed to the fair and equal treatment of all individuals before the law. Further, the EO states:

> [T]raining like that discussed above *perpetuates racial stereotypes and division and can use subtle coercive pressure to ensure conformity of viewpoint.* Such ideas may be fashionable in the academy, but they have no place in programs and activities supported by Federal taxpayer dollars. Research also suggests that blame-focused diversity training reinforces biases and decreases opportunities for minorities....
>
> Therefore, it shall be *the policy of the United States not to promote race or sex stereotyping or scapegoating in the Federal workforce or in the Uniformed Services,* and not to allow grant funds to be used for these purposes. (Italics added)

Section 9 of the EO is clear that the order was "effective immediately," and agency heads were directed to issue guidance on the implementation of the policy.

The following week, on September 28, 2020, OMB issued yet another memorandum (M-20-37) with the subject "Ending Employee Trainings that Use Divisive Propaganda to Undermine the Principle of Fair and Equal Treatment of All."[206] Several weeks later, on October 16, 2020, Secretary of Defense Mark Esper issued implementation guidance in a memorandum titled "Implementation of Executive Order on Combating Race and Sex Stereotyping." In the DoD guidance memorandum, "The DoD Chief Management

Officer (CMO), Secretaries of the Military Departments, and DoD Inspector General (IG)" were directed to "immediately suspend diversity and inclusion training" for all military and civilian personnel.

Regardless of what other Federal agencies chose to do in response to these executive orders, one would think that executive orders issued by the commander in chief would at least stop these trainings from occurring within the uniformed services.

Surprisingly, they did not. At least, not at the base where I am stationed.

Even though large-scale, more public trainings were cancelled—or, more accurately, postponed until after the election results came in—small-group discussions, sponsored by base leadership, continued to be held privately so as to ensure that CRT's radical messaging did not lose its steam. Some of those small-group discussions occurred in the form of reading or book clubs.

In one such discussion that I attended in late-October 2020, the book *So You Want to Talk About Race* was the text that an active-duty servicemember used to facilitate the conversation. I received the invitation to join the discussion in an email that was sent to the entire base.

The black female officer who led the discussion was very respectful—far more so than one might expect given the book's suggestions. She described how difficult it was to choose which book to use as an introduction to the book club. She said, "we" talked a lot about it—whomever *we* were—and indicated to the group that *they* decided Ijeoma Oluo's book was a great first read because it was a soft introduction to the topic of race in America. It appeared that the books that were to follow in the months ahead would somehow present a more direct assault on whites and on the United States than the ideologically possessed, racist, and anti-American rhetoric of Oluo. However, I will leave it to the reader to decide if Oluo's work is a "soft introduction" to discussions on race.

In a special section of the book titled "A Discussion Guide," Oluo suggests ways one might consider facilitating discussions about the book's contents, saying "the comfort of white attendees should be very, very far down on the priority list."[207] In her suggestions regarding creating safe spaces for the discussion, she advocates re-introducing a form of segregation into American society: If whites "feel strongly that they need to center their feelings and experiences in the discussion, set up a space away from the group where they can talk with other white people. Do not let it take over the group discussion or become a burden that people of color in the group have to bear."[208]

In case you are wondering what else military servicemembers and Federal employees were taught from Oluo's book, let me tell you. At this point, you may not be very surprised.

The book teaches that the United States is "a white supremacist society" that must be "dismantled piece by piece."[209] It teaches that speech that makes "people of color feel unsafe" is "an act of violence," but that if whites are uncomfortable, "do not allow [them] to be treated as if harm has been done to them."[210] Oluo's work emphatically teaches other aspects related to CRT, topics such as: "privilege," "intersectionality," "cultural appropriation," "police brutality," and "microaggressions"—all ideas that were specifically prohibited in DoD guidance as a result of President Trump's executive orders.

Oluo goes beyond teaching the ideological concepts of CRT and provides practical suggestions to her readers in order to make an impact in the real world.

For example, in case military servicemembers are at a loss as to which organizations they should be donating their money, the book proposes giving to organizations such as the American Civil Liberties Union (ACLU), Planned Parenthood, and the NAACP.[211] In case military servicemembers are confused about how they should cast their votes during an election year, Oluo instructs readers they should vote for politicians who support raising the minimum wage and who favor police reform.[212] Oluo likely didn't have the uniformed services in mind when she wrote her book, though CRT's proponents must be delighted it has gained traction on military installations. At the time of this writing, I have not yet confirmed whether Oluo's book has made it to the shelves of our military service academies' Diversity and Inclusion reading rooms, where one can find other predominantly Leftist literature about radical Social Justice movements and the evils of America.

The discussion group I attended was not done without the knowledge and consent of the highest-ranking leaders on the base. Oluo's book, and others like it, had been mentioned earlier in an article that was sent by email to the entire base in July 2020. The article we all received by email, written by Daisy Auger-Dominguez (Chief People Officer at VICE Media Group, and Vice-Chair of the board of directors of Planned Parenthood Federation), was titled "Getting Over Your Fear of Talking About Diversity." In the article, Dominguez suggests leaders read certain books to educate themselves about "issues of women, people of color, people with disabilities, LGBTQ+, religious minorities and other marginalized groups." The books Auger-Dominguez recommends include Oluo's *So You Want to Talk About Race* (the book from which I've been quoting), Minda Harts' *The Memo: What Women of Color Need to Know to Secure a Seat at the Table*, Jodi Patterson's *The Bold World*, and Dolly Chugh's *The Person You Mean to Be: How Good People Fight Bias*—all the kinds of books the American people hope their armed forces are reading in their spare time.

Redefining Diversity

Unbeknownst to me and most other servicemembers, decision-makers had determined long ago what the shifting sands of Diversity and Inclusion training within the Defense Department were going to look like.

As early as 2011, during the Obama-Biden Administration, "the Department of Defense *began shifting away from principles of non-discrimination and recognition of individual merit.* The Pentagon's 2011 Military Leadership Diversity Commission (MLDC)," a commission most people in uniform have never heard of, by the way, "largely composed of diversity 'experts' and academics, issued a voluminous report that *re-defined 'diversity' to mean racial and sexual quotas and group rights, not individual rights and meritocracy,*" explains Elaine Donnelly, President of the Center for Military Readiness.[213] (Italics added)

Redefining diversity to mean "racial and sexual quotas and group rights" is not surprising when "experts" and "academics" are given power to determine what matters for America's military. Douglas Murray has pointed out that even back in 2006, a survey showed that 18 percent of academics at US universities self-identified as "Marxist."[214] Nearly a quarter identified as "radical."

Donnelly further details what was in the 2011 MLDC report, and explains how the 2021 National Defense Authorization Act promotes an agenda within our armed forces that is rife with CRT:

> The MLDC report admitted the concept would be difficult for advocates of color and sex "blindness" to grasp: "Successful implementation of diversity initiatives requires a deliberate strategy that ties *the new diversity vision* to desired outcomes via policies and metrics…This is *not about treating everyone the same.*"
>
> The House version of the pending National Defense Authorization Act for 2021 would codify this MLDC agen-

da. Among other things, the legislation would *establish high-level "Chief Diversity Officers" empowered to approve promotions only for officer candidates who embrace critical race theory indoctrination* and fit the desired race, sex, and sexual characteristics.

The House defense bill also would establish a Diversity and Inclusion Advisory Council of the Department of Defense. This panel, or a similar pentagon committee that Defense Secretary Mark Esper plans to establish in December [2020], *likely would push for the critical race theory agenda, demonstrations and indoctrination at military bases,* and swift removal of "racist" monuments and symbols."[215] (Italics added)

Again, what we are seeing is a Diversity and Inclusion industry that is steeped in CRT, which is rooted in Marxism. Sadly, this is what has been called a "moral imperative" and an "operational imperative" for the Defense Department.[216] This is why I said at the beginning of this chapter that I agreed with Carol Swain that the Diversity, Equity, and Inclusion industry is among the greatest threats facing American society. It is, without a doubt, a threat to the good order and discipline of our armed forces.

Theory in Action—The Black Lives Matter Movement

The late Martin Luther King Jr., America's most famous Civil Rights hero, rejected Marxism as a solution to the injustices he saw in society.[217] King critiqued its "ethical relativism, which allowed evil and destructive means to justify an idealistic end. Communism, wrote King, 'robs man of that quality which makes him man,' that is, being 'a child of God.'"[218]

Following his graduate work in theology in the late 1940s and early 1950s, King held to the belief that "communism and Christianity are fundamentally incompatible."[219] He soon became enamored with the life and writings of Mahatma Gandhi and "came to see for the first time that the Christian doctrine of love operating through the Gandhian method of nonviolence was one of the most potent weapons available to oppressed people in their struggle for freedom."[220]

King's nonviolent resistance stands in stark contrast to today's Social Justice activists who claim—as a front—to be fighting for the same cause. The founders of the Black Lives Matter Global Network (BLMGN) reject King's beliefs and approach, preferring instead Marx, Marxism, and violent revolution. In 2015, Black Lives Matter movement co-founder Patrisse Khan-Cullors said that she and her fellow organizers were "trained Marxists."[221] Cullors explained: "*We actually do have an ideological frame. Myself and Alicia [Garza] in particular are trained organizers. We are trained Marxists.*"[222] (Italics added)

Cullors became a trained organizer under the mentorship of communist organizer Eric Mann at the Labor/Community Strategy Center, which she called her first "political home." The Center uses grassroots organizations to "focus on Black and Latino communities with deep historical ties to the long history of anti-colonial, anti-imperialist, pro-communist resistance to the US empire."[223] Mann urges protégés, as "a critical part of this effort," to "read Marx and Engel's *Communist Manifesto*, W.E.B. Dubois's *Black Reconstruction in America*, V.I. Lenin's *What's to be Done?*, Harry Haywood's *Black Bolshevik*...Mao Tse-Tung's *On Practice*..." and to "read as if your life depended on it."[224]

Cullors, who characterizes herself as an "openly queer, social justice activist and movement organizer," references her training in Marxist ideology as if it were a badge of honor and an indication of her *bona fides*—as if violent class conflict is the path to a better world. It is not.

Instead, the admission to being "trained Marxists" is a revelation of the Black Lives Matter movement's ultimate aims of destroying "the existing social and political order." It is an open declaration that "their ends can be attained only by the forcible overthrow of all existing social conditions." The movement is dedicated to dismantling traditional culture, disrupting the nuclear family, and further socializing public education. From the Black Lives Matter website:

We are self-reflexive, *we do the work required to dismantle cisgender privilege* and uplift Black trans folk, especially Black trans women who continue to be disproportionately impacted by trans-antagonistic violence.

We disrupt the Western-prescribed nuclear family structure requirement by supporting each other as extended families and 'villages' that collectively care for one another, *especially our children, to the degree that mothers, parents, and children are comfortable.*

We foster a queer-affirming network. When we gather, we do so with the intention of *freeing ourselves from the tight grip of heteronormative thinking,* or rather the belief that all in the world are heterosexual (unless s/he or they disclose otherwise).[225] (Italics added)

As we already noted, Marxist revolutions historically have not gained much of a foothold in American society. In fact, Americans fought wars against Marxist-communist regimes in order to preserve liberty for ourselves, our allies, and free nations abroad. Other than in small pockets in our university system, Marxism has historically been unpopular, to say the least.

So how does one make a Marxist revolution a possibility in America? How might one give it appeal?

On the main page of the same Black Lives Matter website, we read: "Our fight for *liberty, justice* and *freedom* continues." Note the words. Americans and freedom-loving peoples across the world do not take those ideas lightly. The ideas for which the BLM movement is "fighting" are all principles undergirding America's founding.

What is not to support in such a narrative? The answer: nothing.

And what decent person, especially someone who believes in America's founding principles, would disagree with the assertion that "black lives matter?" The answer: no one.

"Black lives matter" is an irresistible slogan, and it was intentionally designed to be such. Because the slogan is irresistible, revolutionaries weaponize it to their advantage, shaming others who are not willing to bow down and apologize for their privilege or utter compelled phrases under the threat of violence.

Janaya Future Khan (Khan-Cullors' spouse), organizer of Black Lives Matter Toronto, quotes social activist Toni Cade Bambara to explain it in this way: "The role of the artist is to *make the revolution irresistible*....We intend to do just that."[226] [The] Future Khan perfectly captures the essence of that "grand art" referred to earlier by the Illuminists. She understands the necessity of rendering the revolution certain—irresistible; she understands that, as F.A. Hayek observed in his classic *Road to Serfdom*, "the most effective way of making everybody serve the single system of ends toward which the social plan is directed is to make everybody believe in those ends."[227]

When one understands these things about both Marxism and the BLM movement, the rioting, looting, and violence of 2020 come into clear focus, and the polarizing rhetoric assumes purpose. It becomes perfectly clear why certain social injustices mattered a great deal to both the mainstream media and Marxist activists, while the vast majority of other injustices received little or no attention whatsoever. It is because not all lives or injustices matter equally when what one is aiming at is the creation of energy sufficient for the "more or less veiled civil war" to break out into "open revolution."

Marxist organizations are therefore always on the lookout for crises to exploit, and the Black Lives Matter movement masterfully capitalized on—and sometimes created—such crises in 2020. "You never want a serious crisis to go to waste," says American politician Rahm Emanuel. "And what I mean by that [is] it's an opportunity to do things that you think you could not do before."[228]

Other co-founders and organizers of the BLM movement provide us a peek behind the veil. Alicia Garza, the other "trained Marxist" mentioned earlier by Khan-Cullors, wears a noticeable tattoo on her chest. The tattoo is a quote from the last lines of a poem by June Jordan. It reads:

> I am not wrong: Wrong is not my name
> my name is my own my own my own
> and I can't tell you who the hell set things up like this
> but I can tell you that from now on *my resistance*
> *my simple and daily and nightly determination*
> *may very well cost you your life.*

Garza, who asserts that "Black lives can't matter under capitalism," accomplished an internship in 2003 with the School of Unity and Liberation (SOUL), an Oakland-based training program for Social Justice organizers.[229] The school is a Leftist education program whose purpose is to teach "people of color, women, queers, and progressives, how to organize movements and mobilize populations." According to Garza, students at the school learn about "capitalism and imperialism and white supremacy and patriarchy and heteronormativity [*sic*]."[230]

The BLM movement was born of a series of Facebook posts beginning with Garza following the death of Trayvon Martin, and the #BlackLivesMatter catchphrase was soon thereafter to be uttered even by the President of the United States, Barack Obama. In 2014, Garza acknowledged that the movement was a "political project."[231] Later, in a 2015 Facebook post, Garza explained that "#blacklivesmatter is a collective affirmation and embracing of the resistance and resilience of black people....It is a truth that we are called to embrace if our society is to become human again. It is a rallying cry."[232]

In an interview with the *San Francisco Weekly* in 2015, Garza re-emphasized that the movement is a "political project" when she explained that "there's a broader movement that is participating in this movement that has a range of politics." Part of BLM's goal is to "infuse" that broader movement—which, according to the article, consists of Democrats and other black activists—"with *more radical politics.*"[233] [Italics added] This is done, the article explains, in part, "by continuing to put forward an unapologetically anti-capitalist message."[234] One of Garza's concerns, however, was that the movement would be co-opted by the Democrats who "want to reform policing but balk at more radical action." "If you do it the way that some folks do it," Garza explained, "you're going to lose people, because it seems and feels fringe." The *San Francisco Weekly* article continues:

> Interviewer: When I suggested that [Bernie] Sanders had been talking about socialism on the campaign trail, Garza deadpanned, "Has he?"
> Garza: It sounds like he's been talking a lot about being a social democrat, which is still left of where the Democrat party is, but it's not socialism, it's democratic capitalism. *There should be more voices saying, 'this is not actually socialism, and socialism is actually possible in our lifetime, and this is what that looks like.* What you're talking about is nicer, more gentle capitalism, and, you know, you still need some work on foreign policy.'[235]
> (Italics added)

It is clear from Garza's statements that the BLM "political project" has a radical Leftist social and political agenda—like everything else discussed in this chapter, the BLM movement is one of Marxism's many ugly faces. This is critical to both acknowledge and understand, because the movement plays an important role in the overarching social and political impulse that is appearing within the country and the uniformed services.

Notwithstanding its overt political agenda and the legal obligation our military servicemembers have to remain apolitical, the BLM movement has gained acceptance within the Department of Defense, both among individuals as well as at the institutional level. Servicemembers are allowed to support the BLM movement. They are not, however, allowed to criticize it. More on that in the next chapter.

PART III

UNMAKING AMERICA'S MILITARY

THE BURDEN OF EGYPT. Behold, the Lord rides upon a swift cloud, and shall come into Egypt; and the idols of Egypt shall be moved at his presence, and the heart of Egypt shall melt in the midst of it. And I will set the Egyptians against the Egyptians and they shall fight, every one against his brother and every one against his neighbor, city against city and kingdom against kingdom. And the spirit of Egypt shall fail in the midst thereof, and I will destroy the counsel thereof; and they shall seek to the idols, and to the charmers, and to them that have familiar spirits, and to the wizards. And the Egyptians will I give over into the hand of a cruel lord, and a fierce king shall rule over them, saith the Lord, the Lord of Hosts.

Isaiah

CHAPTER 6

THE NEW AMERICAN MILITARY CULTURE

*The chance of imposing a totalitarian regime on a whole peo-
ple depends on the leader's first collecting round him a group
which is prepared voluntarily to submit to that totalitarian
discipline which they are to impose by force upon the rest.*

F.A. Hayek

AFTER LEAVING MY OFFICE ON BASE *and walking from my building out
into the parking lot, I am greeted by the large decals on the rear window
of a white Ford Flex, which read:*

"#BLM," written in large, white, capital letters, and

"SO BACK THE FUCK OFF," written in large, red, capital letters.

*The first time I saw it, it caught my eye from across the parking lot.
There are other decals on the rear window of the car, too, though they
are, as one might imagine, less memorable.*

*While bumper stickers can be offensive, they are not inevitably in-
trusive. Since I am responsible for the well-being of the servicemembers
under my command, I tend to not spend my time focused on the ways
in which bumper stickers might impact the morale of my unit. However,
when somebody's activism begins to find its way into the halls of my own
squadron, it gets my attention.*

*In July 2020, shortly after I took command, one of the base chap-
lains stopped by my office to introduce himself. We had but a brief initial*

introduction. The chaplain explained that it was no longer the Chapel's practice to give office space to their chaplains over in the chapel—that was only how the Chapel used to do things—but that the chaplains were now expected to live amongst and be imbedded in the units they served. He explained that one of the other operational squadrons had already provided him an office space, and that he was also interested in finding a space within my unit.

The chaplain also explained his intent to share his "Race in America" classes with members of my unit. I explained to him that I was on my way out the door, kindly expressed hesitation at his proposal, and said that I would like to sit down with him at some point soon to meet him and learn more about the classes. The chaplain seemed surprised at my hesitation and pursued the issue further. Perplexed by his insistence, I respectfully explained that this was an operations squadron, that we have a mission to accomplish, that there was no greater advocate of the important role of the chaplaincy than me, but that there was also a proper balance between operations and chaplain support that I was interested in finding. At that, he said:

"I have heard about commanders like you, but I've never met one."

While I cannot know for sure what was meant by the chaplain's statement, I considered it a jab. Likely, he meant no insult. But the comment seemed intended to convey the chaplain's dismay at my reluctance to readily welcome his classes (about which I knew little at the time) into my squadron. The chaplain has a friendly demeanor, and though his statement was not said with an angry tone, I could not help but perceive he viewed me as an opponent to whatever it was that he was pursuing, and it left me concerned about our interaction.

Nearly one month later, the chaplain and I met in my office for a follow-up visit. It was our first real sit-down, and the intent was to discuss his classes on race. The conversation lasted for about an hour and fifteen minutes. The chaplain explained that the classes were intended to facilitate dialogue on how we can heal as a nation and as a service, and how we might overcome systemic racism.

I asked him what he meant by systemic racism.

He replied with an unclear vignette, skirting the issue somewhat, and then, after brief hesitation, replied:

"Basically, whites are racist."

I told him I did not believe such a problem existed in our country—at least as he defined it—or within our service and explained to him why I thought such a message not only had no healing power, but that I was concerned it would create division and unhealthy tension between members of my unit where none previously existed.

We discussed these issues at length, and our conversation was, for the most part, professional and respectful despite our differences. During the conversation, the chaplain shared many views which gave me additional cause for concern. Among the most alarming to me were his views that the United States was founded by racists, that American history was written by a white oppressor class that was racist, and that "history must be rewritten."

I expressed my concern over his views. I explained to him that to impugn guilt to members of my unit solely based on the color of their skin epitomized racism.

He disagreed.

I also expressed my concern that the narrative he had chosen to adopt about American history was fueled by a divisive political ideology that was dangerous.

He disagreed.

I also explained to him that his narrative on race and American history undermined the trust our service members place in their oath to support and defend the Constitution.

He disagreed.

Culture in Transition

CULTURES ARE NOT REMADE OVERNIGHT. But there is a new American military culture in the making, and, if current trends are left unchecked, what is now merely emergent will ossify and become the new normal—a new culture.

Culture is the product of certain key beliefs, or of underlying basic assumptions, shared by a group of people. Members of the same culture share the same goals and, therefore, the same values. They share the same cultural narrative, which produces group identity and is like glue that holds people together.

Like the members of any culture, US military servicemembers are knit together by their beliefs and values. For example, servicemembers take an oath to support and defend the Constitution, believing that it is worthy of preservation. Servicemembers share a love of their country—as is expected in a free society with a volunteer force—believing in its fundamental goodness. Their patriotism leads servicemembers to be willing to sacrifice even their own lives in defense of their country, believing such a sacrifice may be necessary to protect liberty.

In addition to the motivational power of the oath and the patriotic spirit of our servicemembers, military culture is the product of codified core values established by each of the services defining their key beliefs or foundational aspirations. For example, Airmen and Guardians are taught that because their services value "Integrity First, Service Before Self, and Excellence in All We Do," they should adopt those values as their own. The common identity and shared purpose of servicemembers are reflected, in part, in the fact that each wears the same uniform and, roughly speaking, adheres to the same dress and grooming standards.

But let us explore the oath a bit further.

The oath servicemembers take to support and defend the Constitution *alone* contains the power that fundamentally shapes America's military culture.

How so?

The oath presupposes the Constitution's virtue—its worthiness. It also therefore implies the justness, correctness, and worth of the system of government instantiated by the Constitution in the first place. The oath is a living confirmation of a particular narrative about what America was in the beginning, since its inception. It takes for granted America's founding philosophy and, thus, implicitly conveys the greatness of the American ideal.

The oath imposes upon servicemembers the burden of providing for the common defense—one of the primary purposes for which the Constitution was written, as described in its preamble. In short, swearing an oath to defend the Constitution is an affirmation that America *was*, *is*, and *should remain* worth defending. It carries motivational power and imposes a shared obligation upon the community of military professionals.

Marxism seeks to undermine belief in *all* of those things. It is, as we have seen, anti-American. When US military servicemembers are taught to believe in Marxism by way of "Diversity and Inclusion" trainings rooted in the tenets of critical race theory, it undermines their trust in their sworn oath to defend the Constitution and begins reshaping the landscape of military culture. *The new culture is the result of different beliefs about what America was, is, and should be.* In the new cultural narrative being promoted broadly in America—and now, even in the military—America was and is racist, white supremacist, and white nationalist, and *should become something altogether different than* what it was and is. This new narrative will, of course, not be believed by many servicemembers and so the force is fractured. Whether or not it is irrevocably fractured remains to be seen.

On top of Marxist propaganda in the form of critical race theory, servicemembers are subtly compelled to accept a Marxist social and political agenda.

How?

When servicemembers are told, for example, that public support for the BLM movement is *not* politically partisan behavior, but that, on the other hand, to criticize or *not* support the BLM movement is tantamount to racism or white supremacy—and is, without question, politically partisan behavior—it pressures servicemembers into accepting a Marxist social and political agenda.[236] After all, even *silence* is tantamount to *violence* according to the neo-Marxist narrative, and is not a suitable position for one to take if they are to be truly "anti-racist." The services thereby not only acknowledge two competing worldviews; they are, in essence, legitimizing the Marxist worldview and demonizing the American.

In his work *Maps of Meaning*, Jordan Peterson explains what is at stake when culture is disrupted in this way, specifically if Western culture is sufficiently threatened so as to undermine its key beliefs. Keep in mind what implications this has for the US military:

> Every culture maintains certain key beliefs that are centrally important to that culture, upon which all secondary beliefs are predicated. These key beliefs cannot be easily given up, because if they are, everything falls, and the unknown once again rules. *Western morality and behavior, for example, are predicated on the assumption that every individual is sacred.* This belief…provides the very cornerstone of Judeo-Christian civilization. *Successful challenge to this idea would invalidate the actions and goals of the Western individual; would destroy the Western…social context for individual action.* In the absence of this central assumption, *the body of Western law…codified morality—erodes and falls.* There are no individual rights, no individual value—and the foundation of the Western social (and psychological) structure dissolves. *The Second World War and Cold War were fought largely to eliminate such a challenge.*[237] (Italics added)

Considered in the context of the obligation of the military servicemember—specifically, the *willing* sacrifice of one's own life in defense of the country—the destruction of the "social context for individual action," as Peterson describes it, easily becomes a serious accession and retention problem for every branch of the US military. Put another way, if the motivational relevance of military service in a voluntary force is destroyed, then the services will have a difficult time recruiting and retaining voluntary servicemembers. This has already begun happening, as will be seen in this chapter.

The uniformed services were once honorably apolitical, or at least politically neutral. Recently, however, they have become hotbeds of a politically partisan training agenda. As a result of increasingly overt support for the progressive, Marxist worldview, servicemembers have been empowered to begin using social media platforms to pursue Social Justice activism without consequence, despite their legal obligations to remain apolitical. These activists use social media to utter public support for radical social agendas and revolutionary aims against the United States and fellow Americans.

As we shall also see, even while progressive social activism goes unchecked by senior leaders, disagreement with the radical views of these activists is being punished by senior leaders. If servicemembers hold views—*actual or assumed*—that are judged to be contrary to the dictates of the Marxist faith—whether the views be political, religious, cultural, or otherwise—they are increasingly demonized and marginalized. Servicemembers are trained that all voices opposed to the revolutionary agenda are "racists," "fascists," "right-wingers," "white supremacists," and "white nationalists," even though, in the overwhelming majority of cases, such is simply not true. These are also particularly ill-placed labels considering there are many non-white servicemembers who hold political, religious, and cultural views contrary to the dictates of progressive social activism.

The Desire to Serve

How would *you* like to serve in a white supremacist military in defense of a systemically racist country?

It sounds like a raw deal and, of course, most would not.

Tragically, too many of our young active-duty servicemembers are beginning to believe that is precisely what they have signed up to do—not because it is true, but because it is what they are being taught.

Recently, Pentagon Press Secretary John Kirby explained that "extremism" is *"not an insignificant problem* within the ranks."[238] (Italics added) The extremism to which he referred is "white nationalism" and "white supremacy," which has become a popular topic of discussion of late.[239] In his confirmation hearing, the newest Secretary of Defense, Lloyd Austin, underscored the need to rid the military of "racists and extremists."[240] The Defense Department, however, has yet to offer data in support of its claim, but has indicated it is determined to find it.[241] As *DoD News* admits, the Defense Department still "needs to figure out what constitutes extremist activity," and still needs to determine *"what is permissible in looking for* extremism within the ranks."[242] (Italics added) Because of these assertions of white supremacist extremism within the ranks, my own squadron just executed a Defense Department-directed "down-day" to have training on the subject.

Within two weeks of the Defense Department's admission that it is in search of data to support its claims of white nationalism, I was notified as a commander of new reporting procedures we were now to follow. Effective immediately, whenever any disciplinary action or administrative paperwork of any kind is issued for an infraction, military leaders are directed to report said disciplinary action to the base legal office, *indicating the race and gender of the recipient of the paperwork as well as that of the leader who issued it.* The new policy clearly signals that the nature and context of the infraction are immaterial. It is merely the race and gender of those involved that matters to the Defense Department. If that is not true, it is at least the perception left with servicemembers. The new policy is a great way to chip away at the morale of an organization.

In my own experience during the past twenty years, military leaders of all ranks have always made it clear that they—and the services generally—have "zero tolerance" for discrimination of any kind. And they have meant it. For that reason, discrimination within the military is infrequent. When exceptions occur and a servicemember is found guilty of discrimination, such behavior is not tolerated—it is punished.

Whether one believes the narrative that the uniformed services are awash with white nationalists, is, at this point, almost becoming inconsequential as it is having a detrimental impact on service-members' desires for continued service. This narrative of white nationalist extremists plaguing the ranks, in combination with the other neo-Marxist, postmodernist, CRT-fueled narratives we have mentioned in earlier chapters, specifically:

that the country *was founded by racists*,
that the country *has always been racist*,
that the *Constitution's ratification codified white supremacy as the law of the land*,
that *whites are inherently racists* (whether they realize it or not), and
that the *country must transform* and become something altogether different than *what it was* and *is*,

is wrecking young people's motivation to serve in the US military, regardless of their political leanings. Many of *those who believe* these false narratives are finding their motivation for continued service shattered. Many of *those appalled by* the accusations are likewise demotivated. These narratives are teeing up a lose-lose scenario for the uniformed services and for the American people. I know because I am hearing about it all the time from people at my own base and elsewhere.

The following are examples of what I am talking about from my own conversations. Of note, I have deliberately left out the names out of the individuals in the stories to preserve their privacy and have also refrained from quoting those conversations verbatim. Their identities are irrelevant. What they say, however, is likely an accurate representation of the feelings of thousands of others. What follows are my words, not theirs.

During his exit interview, one young man that worked for me explained why he no longer desired to serve in uniform.

The bottom line?

He was tired of identity politics. As an Asian-American, it seemed to him the services were strictly concerned with the opportunities and equities of blacks versus whites. From his perspective, the Defense Department lost its interest in him—this, despite his positive experience within our own unit.

Another young man, a graduate of the Air Force Academy, explained to me one day that he and his peers—all stationed at various bases—are all planning to separate following the culmination of their service commitment.

Their reason?

They are tired of the Defense Department teaching servicemembers they are racists solely based on the color of their skin. These young officers do not consider themselves racists, nor have they behaved in ways that would be considered racist by their leaders or their peers.

A mid-level officer emailed me recently saying "hat's off to you for having the stomach to stick around." We are old friends and were previously stationed together but had not stayed in touch. He explained he left active duty because of "the direction the Air Force was heading."

A well-respected senior enlisted leader, a non-white female whose career potential appears unlimited, explained to me that she plans on separating after this assignment because she no longer feels valued in the military based on her work ethic and the quality of her work. Instead, the thought is ever looming in her mind that she is being given opportunities because of her ethnicity and sex. She admits that she does not know if that is the case but cannot be sure. She cannot shake the thought because it is what the services are constantly talking about.

She also admits she is tired of all the talk about racism. As a conservative, she feels she has been lumped in with the elusive white nationalists. Because she does not believe there is a systemic racism problem within the services, she feels that the services consider her to be "part of the problem," not part of the solution they are seeking for the future.

A young female explained to me that she had come to believe she was not only an outsider in her country, but also an outsider in the service.

Why had she come to believe such an isolating and divisive idea?

She admitted she had not been raised by her parents to believe such an idea, and she had not learned it from her friends. Instead, she had recently learned it from the chaplain who had been teaching her and others at the base about "race in America." She was trained to believe that she was an outsider because of the color of her skin, and that people were out to get her—white people. Rather than helping disabuse her of these false notions, the Defense Department is presently confirming them.

Another young man explained that he was beginning to wonder if everything he had been taught growing up was wrong. He explained that he had been raised in a conservative Christian home and possessed a patriotic disposition by nature. He knew that his worldview conflicted with the ideas presented in the base's Diversity and Inclusion trainings, as well as what he saw playing out daily and weekly in the mainstream media. He felt unanchored. He, like so many others, had become a victim of gaslighting.

Was he allowed to hold onto his conservative beliefs, he wondered? Would doing so get him in trouble, or jeopardize his career?

Would he be considered a racist for speaking freely? Or did he need to abandon his views to be considered a decent person and fit in within the service?

Nearly every one of the above stories came to me unsolicited. Some came up during the one-on-one interviews I conducted with every member of my unit shortly after taking command. Others came up during various meetings, such as when a member requested time on my calendar for mentorship, or during routine exit interviews, which I conduct any time a member of my unit is separating or moving to a new assignment. Some are not members of my unit.

During exit interviews, I give members the opportunity to provide parting feedback—whether positive or critical—so that we can improve the way we do business in our unit. During these exit interviews in particular, members are prone to share what they really think, knowing it will be the last time they step foot into the squadron. I mention this only to note that these stories *did not* come to me because I put members on the spot or asked them to divulge their views on American politics. I presume they shared because our unit has fostered an environment of inclusion and trust.

The Space Force, my own service, has many terrific leaders—good people—some of the best I have ever worked with. The problems identified in the above stories are not problems unique to the Space Force, but are problems faced by every branch of the US military and other federal agencies. The reader will recall that President Trump's executive order banning race and sex stereotyping was directed at *all* federal agencies, to include the uniformed services, because these problems are not isolated to specific organizations.

The stories of these servicemembers elevated my concerns and made me curious what was happening outside of my own experience—because despite being unsolicited, they were, after all, only my own experiences. I began reaching out to others I knew. In talking with them about the problems I was seeing, I began discovering many more examples of servicemembers losing their desire for continued service in the wake of the hyper-politicization of the military culture—an environment being shaped by the divisive, Marxist tenets of critical race theory, including the cultural narrative that America is systemically racist and the false notion that whites are inherently racist. Below, I mention only several more examples.

One woman I spoke with, a service academy and military enlistment advisor, explained that her high school seniors were losing their desire to attend the service academies or join the services following graduation. Her students, many of whom were from conservative homes, have shared that they are unsure what their country stands for anymore. Their uncertainty, they say, is a direct result of the kinds of progressive narratives noted above.

Some of my peers, other lieutenant colonels, have shared with me their own uncertainty as to whether they will stay in the service until the twenty-year mark. This means they are considering separation just several years shy of pulling in a pension, a thought they never entertained until the past several months. After having served for so long and spending years away from their families serving wherever and whenever asked, they feel betrayed by the persistent narrative that they contribute to a problem of systemic racism simply because they are white. They, and everyone who has ever worked with them, know that such accusations of racism are baseless.

I have learned of black cadets at the US Military Academy (USMA), or West Point, who are no longer sure they want to graduate and commission in the Army.

The reason?

They are conflicted about swearing an oath to defend a white supremacist country. These young cadets were depressed for days after being trained to believe that the country was not as noble as they once believed.

Despite his reluctance, another black West Point cadet has been pressured by other black students to believe the Marxist lie that whites are predominately racist. He is learning to shrug it off, but he understands that he potentially faces ostracization for *not embracing his blackness.*

Another young man, a cadet at the US Air Force Academy, explained to his sponsor family—a local volunteer family prearranged by the school to provide cadets a weekend getaway and support structure—that "the Air Force Academy is the last place on Earth you want to be if you are a white, Christian male."

Clearly, there are worse places one could be as a white, Christian male than at a US military service academy. But the literal accuracy of his assertion is beside the point. Rather, his remarks are a manner of expression that is a revelation of the emergent culture. It reflects his own perception and feelings—the perception that he is unwelcome because of his race and religious convictions and the feeling or sense of discrimination.

There are many more stories like these. While it is not necessary to present an exhaustive catalogue, it is enough to acknowledge that the above stories reflect a wide-scale reality. The reality is this: the Defense Department's current radical narrative about systemic racism in America and in the services is causing people to lose their desire to serve. This is true for people on both sides of an increasingly polarized political spectrum.

Military Service Academies

The military service academies are assimilating into the progressivism of other universities throughout the country, where identity and race-based politics rule the day and the ideology of victimhood largely defines the campus environment.[243] These influential institutions shape the character and attitudes of many of those who will become our nation's highest-ranking military officers. These leaders in turn influence our nation's policies.[244] We turn first to West Point for a look at its emerging military culture.

In a forty-page policy proposal—a manifesto—dated June 25, 2020, recent graduates of West Point—commissioned officers at the time—decry their alma mater's many "failures," specifically with regards to systemic racism, and issue a "call to action" to "West Point leadership, the Long Gray Line, and the citizens" of the United States.[245] The overt attack on West Point, in which the words *fail, failed*, and *failure* appear nearly forty times in reference to the institution and its leaders, demands that the school "normalize anti-racism" and "radical inclusion," and make it "the lens through which" West Point "executes all of its aims."

The two main activist-scholars promoting accepted definitions of "anti-racism" are Robin DiAngelo and Ibram X. Kendi, with whom our active-duty-activist manifesto authors are no doubt familiar. DiAngelo and Kendi share the view that there is no such thing as "not-racist." According to their argument, for a white woman to assert she is "not-racist" is to reveal her racism. Because she is white, she is racist by virtue of her unavoidable complicity in a system of "whiteness" that she necessarily benefits from. She is therefore faced with a *false* choice: she can be racist and admit her racism—and take up the mantle of "anti-racism"—or she can be racist and deny it.[246] In practice, the demand of these graduates to "normalize anti-racism" at West Point is to establish an institutionalized witch hunt that aims to help you understand why you, too, are likely a racist.

It is not true that there is no such thing as "not-racist." It is actually what an individual *should be* or hope to become. But as Helen Pluckrose and James Lindsay, authors of *Cynical Theories*, explain: the idea "proceeds from a poor but *strategic* and *politically actionable understanding* of racism that is common in the Critical Race Theory literature."[247] (Italics added)

The authors of the 2020 manifesto—comprised of both male and female, and black and white officers—tout their impressive accomplishments at the beginning of their proposal, intending to demonstrate that their words should be taken seriously while unthinkingly confounding their claims that they were unduly oppressed, or that black cadets face institutionally imposed obstacles that white cadets do not. Among the impressive honors listed, these graduates were Valedictorians (yes—plural), Fulbright Scholars, a Rhodes Scholar, a class president, and captains of numerous sports teams. They are talented, credentialed, and woke. But they are not creative. They are merely parrots reciting the same talking points as other ideologically possessed, hand-me-down Marxists. The United States was "founded and built upon white supremacy," they claim. West Point is rife with "intersectional discriminations," and "microaggressions," and "implicit biases," and so on. They accuse West Point's leaders of "duplicity" in that they merely pretend to care for blacks, asserting that there is "no hope for the development of character in a space where Black women are seen as monkeys."

In their effort to achieve an "anti-racist West Point," these Army authors have produced a manifesto similar to the Port Huron Statement (1962), which inspired and justified the formation of Students for a Democratic Society (SDS). The name sounds nice to those unfamiliar with the organization, but it was a socialist student organization with a progressive agenda that had roots in Marxism. In fact, three out of the four drafters of the Port Huron Statement were "red diaper babies," or Marxists.[248] To today's reader, the Port Huron Statement seems like a dull and anticlimactic read.

By 1965, SDS president Carl Oglesby was proclaiming publicly the organization's intention on destroying capitalism.[249] In the several years that followed, activists involved in the organization were busy planning riots "trying to launch" civil war in America.[250] The Port Huron Statement was disingenuous in that it did not openly admit to its socialist agenda. Instead, it called for "participatory democracy"—because who would oppose that?—by which it meant a direct democracy, or "people's democracy."[251] This was precisely how Marx had described the communist future, though the authors of the Port Huron Statement prudently refrained from acknowledging that fact.[252] At its core, it is a document that attempts to preserve the Marxist vision.

The Port Huron Statement was a critique of the social and political system of the United States for failing to achieve international peace and economic justice. Like our Army officer-authored manifesto, it, too, was a call to action. It called for increased government welfare and rejected the widespread anti-communist sentiment of the Cold War. SDS membership eventually swelled to nearly one hundred thousand at its peak. Whereas members initially rallied around cries for "democracy," shortly thereafter they embraced "totalitarian police states like Cuba and North Vietnam and genocidal communist movements like the Cambodian Khmer Rouge."[253] David Horowitz describes in his memoir the natural evolution of groups that promote this vindictive ideology: "In its final spasms of revolutionary fervor, SDS spawned leaders like Bernardine Dohrn and Bill Ayers who called for actual war against 'Amerikkka' and went 'underground' to lead the first political terrorist cult in this country."[254]

The similarity of the West Point graduates' manifesto and the Port Huron Statement is in its use of *politically actionable indictments* of the country and its institutions. The differences, however, between the two are notable. Our Army authors epitomize radical social activism—they are more radical in their language, in their accusations, and in their racism (masked as anti-racism) than were the Marxist authors of the Port Huron Statement.[255] Naturally, then, the views expressed in the "policy proposal" of these active-duty officers are far more divisive than anything in the 1962 statement.

Consider, for example, the demonization of white people. Joy Schaeffer, a white female and valedictorian of her 950-member class, laments the failures of West Point in a section of the manifesto she authored—a section titled "West Point Fails to Teach Anti-Racism"—in the following specific ways:

> I graduated without an understanding of *how I could still be racist, despite my best intentions and the fact that I have always espoused the equality of all people.*
>
> I graduated without an understanding of *how to identify and call out microaggressions,* and that *my silence* in the wake of them enables greater acts of racism.
>
> I graduated understanding the concept of *white privilege,* but not about the specific ways in which it *actively and passively contributes* to the continued marginalization of people of color.
>
> I graduated having learned about the historic "white man's burden," but *without uprooting my own white savior complex.*
>
> I graduated without ever hearing the term "anti-racism."
>
> West Point...did not do enough *to actively reveal and root out the white supremacy that inevitably lies within me as a white person in the United States.*
>
> While being a history major certainly did take sandpaper to *the boulder of my white supremacy,* that is something that many other white cadets never received.
>
> What the current moment has shown us is that *the norm in white America is racism and the supremacy of white citizens* over Black citizens. (Italics added)

Schaeffer concludes her deprecating screed by asserting that "West Point will continue to fail every member of the Army" if it does not become "actively anti-racist," and equip "cadets to be allies"—a catchy Marxist turn of phrase.

Back in 2018, however, just several weeks after she graduated, Schaeffer remembered her experience at West Point in an entirely different light. Expressing her gratitude for the environment at West Point in an interview with a hometown newspaper in Ohio in June 2018, Schaeffer explained: "I'm super proud of the way West Point is fostering an environment where you can talk about issues of gender and race and character."[256]

Schaeffer and the other Army officers weaponize the race dialogue, making it a tool to transform society—seeking to dismantle old society piece by piece, and replacing it with what they hope will be the new America. This is, after all, the purpose of critical race theory. Because woke anti-racist activists will deny the "racist" label as applying to themselves, we will instead call their brand of race-based guilt-by-association "neoracism."[257]

In their ideologically induced rage against whites, Schaeffer and her allies—*neoracists*—have become the very thing they claim to be fighting against, and thereby perpetuate race-based divisions in America and within the Army. Their virtue signaling proves what Thomas Sowell wisely observed about racism, that it is "not dead, but it is on life support—kept alive by politicians, race hustlers and people who get a sense of superiority by denouncing others as 'racists.'"

While the 2020 manifesto is perhaps the most recent public example of student activism at West Point, there were earlier examples. One example is that of Spenser Rapone, class of 2016, who posted pro-communist photos to his Twitter account that gained national attention. In one photo, taken in May 2016 at his West Point graduation ceremony, Rapone raises his left fist while displaying the inside of his wheel cap in the other hand, which reads: "COMMUNISM WILL WIN," in capital letters. A second photo posted by Rapone shows him holding open his service uniform to show that he is wearing a T-shirt displaying a blood-red image of socialist icon Che Guevara.

Rapone, who was later discharged from the Army with an "other-than-honorable" discharge, explained to the *Associated Press* that he tweeted the photos in the fall of 2017 as a show of solidarity with NFL quarterback Colin Kaepernick. In addition to the photos he posted, Rapone had been advocating online for social revolution, and expressing criticism of high-ranking officers and elected US officials.[258] Rapone's case is a reminder that only several years ago the Department of Defense—in this case, the Army—was willing to punish and rid itself of those showing public support for socialist revolutions against the United States. Will it continue to rid itself of socialist revolutionary activists in 2021 and beyond?

The problem of identity politics is not isolated to West Point or its graduates. The Air Force Academy (USAFA), my own alma mater, has also been actively in pursuit. There, though, what made headlines was not the exclusive product of student-activists but was the combined effort of football coaches and players.

In July 2020, the *Colorado Springs Gazette* ran an article titled "Air Force football takes firm social stance with video in support of Black Lives Matter."[259] The article observed that "Air Force football took a definitive side" in the ongoing social movement. And it had. The short three-minute video to which the article referred was posted on the football team's Facebook page and has been available since then until the present.

In the video, "institutional discrimination" is the theme, and football coaches and players assert that "black lives *have not been* and *are not* treated as equals in our society." The offensive line coach, Steed Lobotzke, borrowed from the same CRT-fed talking points used by the West Point graduates by explaining that it is "not enough for us to be 'not-racist.'" The assistant defensive line coach, Del Cowsette, followed Lobotzke by adding, "It's time to be anti-racist"—a call to action which was repeated by others in the video. "It's time to recognize my bias," another asserted. He, of course, was a white coach.

The specific phrase "black lives matter" is said at least seven times in the video, often in an aggressive tone and, as the *Gazette* noted, in a manner that implied "firm" and "definitive" endorsement of the Black Lives Matter movement. The head coach, Troy Calhoun, said the "aim" of the video was to "tell the country and the world" of the team's definitive endorsement of Black Lives Matter—and also, incidentally, to let the world know there are serious "education" and "healthcare" reforms needed in the United States, which the team also happens to mention. Nevertheless, one should not become confused and think the video has anything to do with politics, or "Marxism," as the head coach points out.

Seeing the football team's social and political activism in the online video, a group of Air Force veterans and USAFA alumni were upset enough about its divisiveness that they fought to have it removed. They exchanged literally hundreds of emails with leaders at the Academy from football coaches to the athletic director, to the Superintendent, Lieutenant General Jay Silveria. Meeting with resistance, the group decided to file a formal complaint with the Office of the Air Force Inspector General.

On September 14, 2020, the complaint was filed by Attorney Michael T. Rose, who represented the group. Rose became well-known for his key role in ending "the silence" at West Point in 1973 and has spent decades fighting unconstitutionally discriminatory practices in the services since then. The group's formal complaint appropriately links the Black Lives Matter movement to Marxism, noting also that certain specific language used by the football team in the video—the vocabulary of critical race scholars—had been prohibited by President Trump's September 22, 2020 executive order (see Chapter 5).

The response came two months later. In a memorandum dated November 13, 2020, Rose and the group received a response from the Inspector General's office. The short letter explained that neither the video nor the views expressed therein were in violation of Air Force Instructions, Department of Defense Directives, *or the*

President's Executive Order. "Accordingly," the memorandum states, "there is insufficient evidence to indicate wrongdoing and an inadequate basis to warrant further investigation. We are therefore dismissing your complaint." As support, the memorandum also cited the determination made by the US Office of Special Counsel (OSC) in its July 10, 2020 memorandum titled *Black Lives Matter and the Hatch Act,* which states that the Black Lives Matter Global Network "has not previously been involved in partisan political activity" and is "not...a partisan political group."[260]

In case you missed it, read that last sentence again.

At length, the group (now calling itself STARRS, which stands for "Stand Together Against Racism and Radicalism in the Services") secured a meeting with the current Superintendent, Lieutenant General Richard Clark, and a team of retired Generals invited as guests of the Superintendent. The aim in meeting was to help the Superintendent and Academy leadership understand why the video was divisive and to explain the Marxist roots of the BLM movement. During the December 2020 Zoom meeting, General Clark agreed to remove the video, explaining that it would be replaced with a new video. (At the time of this writing—March 29, 2021—the old video is still publicly available to view on the Air Force Academy football team's Facebook page.)

Ever since the Academy posted the video online, I am informed that longtime donors have discussed withdrawing financial support from the institution and season ticket holders have turned in their tickets, saying they will no longer support USAFA football if it insists on becoming a propaganda arm for the progressive agenda.

Lastly, we turn to the third well-known service academy—the Naval Academy (USNA), or Annapolis. In an apparent demonstration of double standards by the Defense Department and the Navy that has been on display in various news media outlets, a senior midshipman named Chase Standage was under threat of expulsion for what USNA Superintendent, Vice Admiral Sean Buck, called "unsettling" and "callous" social media posts. Indeed, they were. But the real question lurking behind the posts was whether Standage was threatened with expulsion for those reasons or for something far more troubling: the command's disagreement with the content of Standage's speech on ideological grounds, a dislike amounting to viewpoint discrimination in violation of the First Amendment.

Standage's posts commented on race, police, social unrest, and the government's response to that unrest—the kind of emotionally charged social and political issues it is wise for servicemembers to avoid altogether.

The week prior to Standage's tweets that landed him in hot water, USNA midshipmen received guidance in an email dated June 1, 2020, "with regard to conduct online and protesting" in response to the widespread demonstrations and riots following the death of George Floyd. The email, titled "14th Co. Resources and Guidance regarding George Floyd Protests," indicated that midshipmen such as Standage were "allowed to post/like/share stories, pictures, etc. of *partisan nature*, however it must be clear _that these are not the opinions of DOD/USNA/Navy_." (Underlining in original email)

Like many others, Standage found himself caught up in the ensuing emotion that accompanied the social media frenzy. For example, on June 10, 2020, President Donald Trump posted a tweet stating: "Domestic terrorists have taken over Seattle, run by Radical Left Democrats, of course. LAW & ORDER!" From his home in California, where he was staying for the summer, Standage retweeted the President's post from his personal Twitter account adding: "Law and Order from 25,000 ft.," accompanied by an image containing the crosshairs from the view of an aerial camera.[261]

The next day, Standage, who never identified himself as a USNA midshipman or military servicemember, tweeted: "This is why the AGM-114 was invented. I've never seen a more incompetent handling of violent, radical insurgents."[262] His tweet no doubt referred to the HELLFIRE family of missiles used as the primary air-to-ground weapon by the Army, Marines, and Air Force.

Standage responded to another tweet wherein someone advocated for the reduction of funding to police departments. In reply, Standage responded: "Go ahead, cut funds to the police. Community policing is expensive and timely, anyways. Bullets, on the other hand, are cheap and in ready supply."[263] The emotional connection Standage experiences in police-related dialogue is the result of his parents' line of work—both are career Los Angeles Police Department officers. Standage alleges that "in June 2020, his parents responded to looting, vandalism, and rioting that was prompted by social unrest in connection with alleged police brutality towards persons of color."[264] According to United States District Court Judge Ellen Hollander, "Standage believed that his parents worked at great personal risk, as protestors 'threatened to overtake a police station,' made 'plans to raid officers' homes,' and attacked police officers 'with rocks, bottles, bricks, urine and other means.'"[265]

There were other tweets in June 2020 that came under scrutiny, some of which were partially quoted by various news media sources across the country. In response to a tweet about Antifa violence and its occupation of Seattle, Standage replied: "All it takes is one drone strike...."

In another tweet directed to the Mayor of Los Angeles, someone stated: "Do you remember letting police officers kill unarmed people?" Standage replied: "If he let them do that, these riots would've been over a whole lot quicker."[266]

Standage also tweeted comments in response to characterizations of the experiences of black Americans. For example, an individual posted a tweet stating: "Black people have lived with NOTHING but adversity, when their forefathers were forced into labor to make white men rich, they must have amassed a whole lot of character." Standage tweeted in reply: "Splendid, then they should also have good work ethic and no need for welfare programs."

These tweets and others that were tweeted over the course of one week became the subject of investigation. According to Standage, in an interview with the Superintendent as part of the investigation that followed, he was asked if his parents "ever expressed the desire to enact death and violence on protestors," to which Standage took offense.[267] In the end of that same interview, Standage was told that his true character was "deeply flawed and unfixable," and that his "lack of concern for humanity was troubling, and that 'no amount of time will fix the ideals [he was] raised upon.'"[268] Standage's attorney claims that "the Superintendent concluded, without basis, that [Standage's parents'] viewpoints regarding law and order are incontrovertibly 'wrong' and morally flawed, a political viewpoint fueled by the anti-police, racial injustice ideology the Superintendent was espousing and indoctrinating at the Naval Academy."[269]

Based on his tweets, Standage was accused of "racism and racial insensitivity." A *Change.org* petition to the USNA Superintendent was created that said, in part: "[Standage's] continued presence at the Academy and as a member of the military creates an environment of accepted prejudice that *harms midshipmen of color* and the entire brigade."[270] (Italics added)

Meanwhile, other midshipmen, including those of color, had taken to Twitter calling for Standage's ouster and even insinuating his looming death. One such tweet from the class president stated: "The Naval Academy has to make an example out of this kid. I won't stand for anything less." Another midshipman retweeted it, stating: "Go for the jugular. You are class president. Leaders lead."

Another tweet asked: "You ever seen a dead body?!?"

This rhetorically threatening question was retweeted by a black female midshipman, saying: "Competent MIDS to Chase Standage"—meaning, presumably, that any competent, woke midshipman would ask it of Midshipman Standage, implying a threat on his life.

During the same timeframe as Standage's controversial tweets, this same female midshipman retweeted in response to violent riots that were underway in Kentucky: "I hope They burn down the entire city of Louisville." And, in response to another tweet that said, "me watching Louisville burn tonight," with an accompanying video of an excited black female playing with hair spray and a lighter, this female midshipman responded: "me waiting because I know Baltimore pullin [*sic*] up."²⁷¹

The female midshipman's violent hopes were echoed by other midshipmen in various unrelated posts. In response to a tweet from politician and activist Stacey Abrams revealing that Democrats had outvoted Republicans in the final count for Georgia's primaries, a black male midshipman posted: "This is wtf I'm talking about! Let's fucking goooo! Get these old white men outta office. Change starts with us my people."

This same male midshipman, like Standage, had something to say about the government's handling of violent rioters, only his tweets were explicitly racist. In response to a June 9, 2020 tweet from *The Hill* that stated, "US faces allegations of human rights abuses over treatment of protesters," this midshipman tweeted: "We need all countries putting pressure on these white men who have the power in the US. Force them to reform or resign." In another of his retweets, this midshipman criticized the sitting President— unlawful behavior, and punishable under the Uniform Code of Military Justice (UCMJ)—and equated him with Hitler. His tweet stated: "Leaders who have hidden in a bunker and gassed their own citizens include Saddam Hussein, Adolph Hitler and Donald Trump."²⁷²

Amidst all the swirl of social media activism, Standage and his lawyer awaited word from the Office of the Assistant Secretary of the Navy for Manpower and Reserve Affairs about the Navy's decision regarding the USNA Superintendent's recommendation that he be expelled.

On December 30, 2020, the call came from the Assistant Secretary's counsel, advising attorney Jeff McFadden, a USNA graduate himself, that Midshipman Standage was going to be retained in the service and allowed to graduate from Annapolis, and a memorandum was signed by the Assistant Secretary to that effect. However, following the January 6, 2021 Capitol breach by a mixed group of Trump supporters and Antifa agent provocateurs, a sudden reversal was made to the Navy's previous decision.[273]

Four days after the Capitol breach, an *ad hominem* article was published in an Annapolis newspaper, the *Capital Gazette,* calling for "[Sean] Spicer and [Chase] Standage" to be ousted with Trump.[274]

On January 13, 2021, only three days after the appearance of the *Gazette* article, the Assistant Secretary's counsel once again called McFadden informing him that the Navy was reversing its decision in the Standage case, and that he was to be expelled.

According to public legal documents, on January 15, 2021, Secretary of the Navy Kenneth Braithwaite himself signed a new memorandum stating that Midshipman Standage was to be separated from the Naval Academy, thus usurping the separation authority he had previously delegated to the Assistant Secretary in violation of Defense Department regulation and procedure.[275] The old memorandum that had previously been signed by the Assistant Secretary appears to have then been stamped "PREDECISIONAL"—a move intended to indicate that there never really had been any decision made by the Navy prior to Secretary Braithwaite's latest decision. Though signed on January 15th, the Secretary's memorandum was not provided to McFadden until after the inauguration on January 20, 2021, in what appears to be a deliberate attempt to prevent Standage from appealing to former President Trump for pardon.

Standage's lawyer asserted that the "fatally arbitrary" reversal had "everything to do with political ideology, political expediency, political intrigue, and political cowardice—and nothing to do with the rule of law."[276] A motion filed for injunctive relief stated:

It cannot plausibly be argued that the Secretary of the Navy's sudden reversal of his previous decision to retain MIDN Standage is anything other than "fatally arbitrary." The reversal came after an attack piece, attempting to smear MIDN Standage with the brush of last week's terrible events at the Capitol, was planted in an Annapolis newspaper. Moreover, and as set forth in the [Third Amended] Complaint, Defendants engaged in a conscious, deliberate course of action to punish and separate MIDN Standage *based solely on the political and cultural unacceptability of his views, to ignore the law and even the most basic requirements of procedural due process, to virtue-signal their own purported alliance with certain political movements* and ideologies both inside the Naval Academy and sweeping across the Country, and to distance themselves from their President and Commander-in-Chief to avoid criticism in the media and in the public eye generally.[277] (Italics added)

McFadden also noted in court filings that two weeks after Secretary Braithwaite's reversal of the Assistant Secretary's decision regarding Standage, Braithwaite announced publicly he is considering a run for the US Senate seat in Pennsylvania currently occupied by Senator Pat Toomey.[278]

Finally, after a February 12, 2021 court hearing on Standage's motion to preliminarily enjoin the Navy from disenrolling him from the Naval Academy, the court issued its February 19, 2021 order denying Standage's request.[279] Notwithstanding, in the court's order, United States District Court Judge Hollander made it clear in her ruling that, although the court was denying Standage his requested relief *at this time*, he had demonstrated a substantial likelihood of prevailing against the government in any future trial.[280] Specifically, among other findings, she found the government had violated its established procedures of delegating such final disenrollment decisions regarding Navy midshipmen to the Assistant Secretary, that the Naval Academy's decision to disenroll Standage was arbitrary and capricious, and that the Navy had violated Standage's rights to appear before Naval Academy decisionmakers with counsel.[281]

Shortly thereafter, the Navy entered into a settlement with Midshipman Standage, providing, among other things, that he be retained at Annapolis and graduate upon successfully completing a 10-week remediation training program. Barring any disqualifying conduct, Standage will be allowed to graduate with his classmates.

While in my judgment Standage's tweets were inappropriate, more troubling still is that the Naval Academy and senior leaders turn a blind eye to the progressive political activism of his peers, revealing the services' present partisan bias and agenda. It is an "unsettling" and "callous" double standard.

Good Intentions, Orwellian Outcomes

Life at our military service academies has never been easy—in fact, it is a difficult time for most. After completion of the first and second school years, only those cadets truly driven to be there will remain. As senior leaders acquiesce to the demands of activist purveyors of the progressive agenda, they have to ask themselves how it will impact the culture of the academies, the recruitment and retention of cadets in the near-term, and the character of the country's future military leaders in the long-term. Those questions are never easy to answer, but what we are examining in this book can assist in an honest and proper assessment.

By way of brief caveat, we must also note the following. Having criticized the cultural transformation that is underway within the uniformed services, it is necessary to acknowledge the fact that there are decent people actively engaged in what we might term Inclusion initiatives who are trying to ensure the services do not foster environments of discrimination. The desire to eliminate illegal discrimination is inherently noble and, inasmuch as it is sincere, reflects the best in mankind. Many of the people engaged in these efforts are genuine in their concern for others—that has been true in the past and remains true today. The critique here is not meant to spurn the intentions of such people.

However, it is noted that they labor under a false pretext that must be exposed—one that combines actual, relevant data with a destructive Marxist narrative of humanity generally and America specifically. Rather than assisting those who are the true victims of discrimination—and such victims do exist of every demographic—these ideologically sullied efforts *minimize their victimization*, asserting instead that the complaints of ungrateful, entitled, and peevish party activists have equal standing. Thus, even with the best of intentions it is possible they will not achieve their aim of eliminating hatred, discrimination, injustice, and division. On the contrary, enforced outcomes, identity politics, ideologies of victimhood, and sex and race stereotyping are certain to ensure these evils become permanent fixtures within society.

While Midshipman Standage was in danger of being expelled for his social media posts, a different standard appeared in play for others across the services, and, as we have seen, even at the Naval Academy. The hypocrisy reminds one of George Orwell's memorable line from his classic allegorical novel *Animal Farm*, which is intended to convey the sinister double standards of Stalin's communist regime.

In the story, the farm animals conspire to take back control of their farm from the oppressive humans. The leaders of the animal movement establish "commandments" that the animals must follow in order to prevent reproducing the oppressive behavior of the humans. Their creed is the noble affirmation: "All animals are equal"—new society will be more just and fair than the old. However, once society's transformation is in full swing, that noble affirmation is unexpectedly altered by those who assert power in the new society. The corrupted creed is Orwell's warning to our generation. The quest for radical equality always ends in the same way: "All animals are equal but some animals are more equal than others."

Servicemember Social [Media] Activists

Wading through the heaps of radical social and political activist material posted on social media by servicemembers is overwhelming. Much of it is, in a word—extremist. This radical political activism, some of which is plainly rooted in Marxist ideology, has become a favorite pastime for servicemembers across a diverse demographic. Its prevalence makes it easy to find. Yet, it is not the kind of extremism for which the Defense Department is on the hunt.

Even as the DoD insists upon greater diversity and equity—and by this it means diversity based on demographics of race, gender, and sexual preference and enforced equality of outcomes—it will have a difficult time removing from the services black, female, and LGBTQ+ servicemembers who engage in political activism in violation of their legal obligations. Furthermore, the current insistence that these minority groups are already unfairly treated by whites stifles any impetus many white leaders may have to even look for such activism. For that reason alone, some of these activists are likely to continue to abuse their obligations without consequence. Some of them have even said as much online.

For example, explaining why it is not possible to separate his personal life from his professional life, one active-duty lieutenant colonel explained on his Facebook account: "When you look like me...asking me to leave my personal life at the door adds insult to an injury that began when my first ancestors set foot on these lands over 400 years ago...we CAN'T leave ourselves at the door. So buckle up...."

He appears to have meant it when he said to "buckle up." In the past year alone, this member has posted hundreds of times, and *hundreds of those posts* were related to politics.

The lieutenant colonel is black and gay, and he reminds his readers that his own oppression—which, according to him, is the immediate result of his identities—gives him the right to critique elites, despite his obligations as an active-duty servicemember. "In truth, Black, brown, and LGBTQ+ people—particularly Black and trans people—can now critique elites publicly and hold them accountable socially," he explained on Facebook.

Whether one likes it or not, the evidence suggests he is correct.

But in addition to merely "critiquing elites," this officer is an incessant social, political, and cultural critic, and everything one might imagine pertaining to "old society" is fair game. For example, commenting on the BLM and Antifa violence in the summer of 2020, he explained: "If you're wondering when these protests end and what better looks like, you need to understand the problem and act. America has a race problem, it is systemic…so where does it all end? *When we burn the system to the ground.* And WE can, all of us." (Italics added).

Soon thereafter, this servicemember activist posted a link to a video of "the best talk he'd heard in a long time," delivered in Atlanta by rapper Michael Santiago Render, popularly known as Killer Mike. In his speech, Killer Mike, who wore a T-shirt with the words "KILL YOUR MASTERS" on it, said he "woke up wanting to see the world burn down yesterday," referencing the death of George Floyd which had occurred several days earlier. "We don't wanna see targets burning," criticizing the uncalculated efforts of angry rioters in burning down local shops and their own homes, "we wanna see the system that sets up for [*sic*] systemic racism burnt to the ground." Then, in what could understandably be interpreted as an incitement to violence, Killer Mike encouraged blacks to exercise their "political bully power," by "going to local elections and beating up the politicians that you don't like." He further explained: "Now is the time to plot, plan, strategize, organize, and mobilize"—advice he repeated several times during his speech. He apologized for not having more to say, mentioned that he did not really want to be there giving the speech, threw in that we have "a dumb ass President," as well as a few other inspiring words, and turned the time over to others. Again, it was the best speech this lieutenant colonel had heard in a long time.

Referencing Killer Mike's speech, the lieutenant colonel explains: "So America has a race problem. The military has a race problem...Despite America's problems and the military's problems...we CAN change this system; we can...'burn it to the ground.'"

We pause here to ask a question of the Department of Defense: Is this not the language of extremism?

Perhaps more shocking than the fact that individuals have these beliefs and share them publicly, is the amount of public support peers and other leaders in the military are willing to show for such posts. Leaders, commanders even, wrote to thank this officer for his political activism and "liked" his posts. Such public support continues day after day, week after week, month after month.

Though there are far too many posts from this officer to relate here, we mention just several more themes to paint a fuller picture. His flavor of social and political activism is not unique to him, after all. He just happens to be producing more of it than most. A survey of his posts gives us a glimpse into the kinds of statements being posted, shared, and read by literally hundreds of thousands of servicemembers and citizens across the world.

In one post, this officer accuses the military of having "a racially and sexually biased promotion system" (this, in fact, may be true, but likely not in the way he imagines).

In another, he explains how irredeemably racist America is because of the fact that "systemic superiority [was] bred into the DNA of this nation."

In another post, in response to Associate Justice Amy Coney Barrett's Supreme Court confirmation and swearing in, he says: "It's time for us to kick ass and take names. Bring it!"

In other posts, he criticizes policies of the Trump Administration, insists that the positive jobs reports are a deception, that black voters are facing unfair obstacles compared to whites, criticizes the White House trade advisor's views on a manufacturing stimulus, and frequently criticizes the police.

He posts that the BLM movement, whose protests and riots were maybe the largest—and also among the most damaging—in US history, is perhaps "one of the finest examples of patriotism in modern America." The article from which he quoted explained that "the protestors who flooded the streets exemplify the revolutionary spirit of America just as much as the white colonists in powdered wigs."

In other posts, he explains that "for anyone who thinks today's 'cancel culture' has gone too far, you clearly live in a world of privilege." This cancel culture that everyone is kvetching about is not even the real thing, he explains. The real thing is "annihilation, conquering, oppression." His explanation is meant as an accusation against those he considers the ruling class—after all, the ruling class is guilty of those things. What he fails to recognize is that the divisive ideological rhetoric he and other activists employ is often what leads to oppression and annihilation.

This lieutenant colonel makes it clear that "looking like he does" requires him to work "twice as hard" as whites in the military workplace in order to remain on equal footing. Put another way, he avers that whites work only half as hard as he does to achieve the same outcomes. That could be interpreted a number of ways, though his meaning is clear. In any case, we cannot be sure he really believes that. Perhaps he does. When people say things like that—things they have heard others say before that they are merely echoing—they do not often think through what it is that they are actually saying; what it is that they actually mean by it.

To be fair, this officer's sentiment is not unlike some of the comments made by the Air Force's senior leaders—who have served far longer than he has—to which he and others have paid close attention during the past year. Terrible burdens have been shouldered by black servicemembers in the past, immense barriers overcome. The persistence, dedication, and success of such servicemembers in the face of those barriers provides an example to *all* servicemembers. For example, the Air Force Chief of Staff, General Charles Q. Brown, Jr., who is also a black Airman and the first black Air Force Chief of Staff in history, made similar comments as the lieutenant colonel in a video he released titled "What I'm Thinking About?"[282] In the video, General Brown shared that he was thinking about how he has had to work "twice as hard" to prove that his leaders' "expectations and perceptions of African Americans were invalid."

In another of his Facebook posts, the lieutenant colonel references a report called the Independent Racial Disparity Review (IRDR), released by the Air Force in December 2020, to prove that the military has a "persistent and consistent" racial bias problem against black Airmen.

But, in fact, the report does not prove what he claims.

The 150-page IRDR was specifically focused on reviewing "discipline and opportunity" regarding black servicemembers. The IRDR confirmed racial *disparities* exist for black servicemembers in "apprehensions, criminal investigations, military justice, administrative separations," and, consequently, in promotion opportunities and in attendance at military professional education opportunities. Race was a "correlating factor," the report says, but *did not* indicate causality. In other words, the report did not and cannot tell you *why* racial disparities exist—only that they do. That is why the IRDR's Introduction is quick to acknowledge (on page 1) that "while the presence of disparity alone is not evidence of racism, discrimination, or disparate treatment, it presents a concern that requires more in-depth analysis."[283] And so it does.

Another servicemember activist, also a black officer, posted this in light of the death of Republican politician Herman Cain: "F-CK him…he died cooning." His "cooning" reference was an insult based on Cain's having contracted COVID-19 at a Trump rally.

Another posted the following in light of the January 6, 2020 Capitol breach: "You hardcore Trumpers best believe I have been browsing your pages…you are complicit in this stain on our legacy…Liberty and Justice for All…not just people who look like you! Reflect on your part in tonight's events…You cats that truly bought into all this garbage, I hope you feel ashamed." The post was "liked" by many other servicemembers, including leaders.

These social media posts are but drops in a pond. We need not look at more. They all look and smell the same, which is what happens when people cannot think for themselves. By now, you should be far more capable of recognizing ideologically motivated utterances than you were at the beginning of the book.

Let us give the last word to our prolific lieutenant colonel activist. In a Facebook post from January 2021, he posted an article titled: "Arizona GOP lawmaker introduces bill to give Legislature power to toss out election results." Besides being overtly politically partisan, his post mentions "the insanity that has gripped an unfortunately large segment of our society," referring specifically to conservatives, Republicans, and Trump supporters—more than clear if one followed his social media posts throughout 2020. Referencing that "large segment of our society," he continues his bombast by stating emphatically: "[S]o many of these people have a date with destiny and destiny's name is 'New America.'" His "New America" is the "transformed" America sought for by the Marxist BLM co-founders and other progressive activists and leftist politicians in the country who use similar language.

In the last line of his post, he delivers a warning to both his fellow servicemembers as well as to the American people whose personal political views differ from his own. He concludes:

"You can run but you can't hide."

Are you aware of a time in US history when active duty service-members could vow threats upon the American people and face no consequences?

Just what kind of extremists and radicals is the Department of Defense seeking to rid from its ranks? Besides the "white," conservative kind, are there others?

As he noted on his Facebook page, it is probable that due to his race and sexual orientation this servicemember feels protected from the severe consequences a servicemember might expect for such an egregious display of politically partisan activism. And it is probable that his own chain of command, who, considering the constancy of the servicemember's social media presence is undoubtedly aware of his political activism, is hesitant to discipline the member for the same reasons.

Reading through these and many other posts from active-duty servicemembers, one becomes disheartened and angered. It is difficult to retain hope that our social, political, and cultural divide will heal anytime soon when the services allow for their members to become entangled in the political and ideological polarization that is wreaking havoc across the country. The adamance of radical progressives that other Americans bend to their worldview is becoming a potent cultural force that shows no signs of waning. To tolerate it is contrary to the Defense Department's stated aim of creating an inclusive workplace. We must not bestow our approbation upon those who are accelerating the Marxist veiled civil war in the United States.

Accountability in the New Culture

It remains to be seen whether so-called underserved and protected identity groups will be held to the same standards of conduct as other servicemembers. To many, it appears there is a growing imbalance in the administration of discipline and accountability—the story of Midshipman Standage alone bears this out.

As I wrote this chapter, BLM activists were marching on Washington, DC chanting: "Burn it down!"[284] Weekly, there are news articles reporting the same behavior across the country. Servicemembers are rooting them on. In its attempt to rid the ranks of extremists, will the Defense Department purge those who want to "burn down" old society? Will those who advocate "dismantling" America "piece by piece" be brought to account? What about those who issue threats to their fellow Americans via social media? If not, why not?

Perhaps the question is bigger than that of underserved and protected identity groups. Maybe the better, more comprehensive question is: Will servicemembers with progressive views be held to the same standards as non-progressives? Or will progressive social and political activism continue to be permitted in the military while conservative views and values are increasingly scrutinized, ridiculed, and falsely labeled as racist, fascist, and white nationalist?

Why is it that despite increased rhetoric touting the importance of equality, servicemembers sense a looming injustice and unbalanced approach to accountability? It is because in this newly emerging American military culture, the drive for equality means forced inequality. Hayek had it right in his *Road to Serfdom*, written in the shadows of Hitler's totalitarianism and in the wake of global conflict that ushered in the Cold War, when he explained that "even the striving for equality…can result only in an officially enforced inequality—an authoritarian determination of the status of each individual in the new hierarchial [*sic*] order—and that most of the humanitarian elements of our morals, the respect for human life, for the weak, and for the individual generally, will disappear."[285]

CHAPTER 7

THE WRATH TO COME

*The way in which [Americans] have made their appearance
on the scene is quite extraordinary: six months ago nobody
suspected anything and now they appear all of a sudden
in such organized masses as to strike terror into the whole
capitalist class. I only wish Marx could have lived to see it.*

Friedrich Engels, June 3, 1886

WHILE I WAS WRITING THIS BOOK, *and anticipating writing this last
chapter, Tucker Carlson did his evening show on Tuesday, January 19,
2021. It was the evening before Inauguration day. I don't normally watch
Tucker's show, or any other television for that matter, but a friend who
knew that I was writing the book brought it to my attention.*

I was dismayed by what I watched!

*Tucker's show revealed a qualitative decay in Leftist rhetoric towards con-
servatives in our country. It seemed to have happened so quickly—it had
become much worse even in the several months that I had been working
on this book. The progressive Left's appalling invective had reached an
unbelievably low, mean, and accusatory state. I recognized that kind of
speech. It was the ideologically possessed rhetoric of genocide.*

*I had always intended the final chapter of this book to be a warn-
ing—a warning that ideas have consequences. A warning that post-*

modernist, neo-Marxist ideology employs vile rhetoric that stokes rage and leads people to do terrible things. *This chapter is about fratricidal and genocidal warfare, and all of the horror that implies—because you cannot persist in the hate-filled demonization of entire groups of people based on their race or political affiliation without incurring the wrath of genocide. To persist means that it is not a question of whether it will turn into violence—that it will, follows like the night the day. Rather, the only question remaining is when. Unfortunately, neither you nor I control that.*

Below, I have included the pertinent parts of the transcript from Tucker's show that evening. Again, the reason his remarks are relevant is because they reveal the rhetorical demonization of conservatives and whites in the country. It is specifically the kind of rhetoric necessary to justify violence against people.*

[Begin transcript] Good evening, and welcome to "Tucker Carlson To-night." It's weird to say it, but this is the last day of the Trump adminis-tration. If you supported Donald Trump that's a sad thing to face after four years. On the other hand, if you didn't support Donald Trump, if you are one of the many of our professional class who have made hating Donald Trump the very center of your life, this has got to be a pretty good day for you. You won! Your party now has control of everything. By tomorrow afternoon, Donald Trump will be gone for good. You got exactly what you wanted. You should be thrilled about that! You ought to be celebrating!

But they're not celebrating. That's the remarkable thing. No one in the Democratic party seems happy tonight. They're angrier than ever. Instead of taking victory laps, they are plotting revenge against the people they just beat. They're thinking of new ways to injure and humiliate and

---

* I have chosen to include large portions of the transcript simply for context. The words contained herein regarding various elected officials are not mine, but those of Tucker Carlson. In quoting Tucker in context, I am neither agreeing nor disagreeing with his views. I am only interested in the rhetoric employed by those individuals to which he refers.

*degrade their political opponents, make it impossible for them to work
again, throw them in jail, destroy their lives.*

*It's hard to describe how weird and strange and awful this is to watch.
Imagine winning a tennis match in straight sets, then immediately leaping
over the net and smashing your opponent in the face with your racket.
It wasn't enough for you to win. You had to inflict physical pain. You
couldn't be happy until another human being screamed in agony.*

*What kind of person would do that? Well, the kind of people we're
watching now. The kind of people who are even more vicious when they
win.*

*The leaders of the Democratic party have now decided that 74 million
Trump voters weren't just wrong or misguided; they didn't simply back
the wrong guy, or have incorrect opinions, or fail to see the obvious truths.
No! The threat they pose is graver and more serious than that—more
dangerous. These 74 million Trump voters are in fact terrorists. They
are looming, physical threats to the rest of us, and we must deal with
them in the way that you deal with threats like that—existential threats
to the Nation.*

*Saddam Hussein, al-Baghdadi, Kim Jong Un—Donald Trump's
voters.*

*For years, they've told us this country had been infiltrated by Rus-
sian spies, but now we know it's worse than that. The real threat, the
actual enemy, is within—in the end, it always is. Seventy-four million
deviationists lurk in our midst. They look like normal people, but ladies
and gentlemen, do not be deceived. They are Trotskyites. They are wreck-
ers—kulaks! We must root them out. It will take a war to do that—an
actual war—a war on our own people.*

*To make that point as clear as possible, the Democratic party has
marshalled military leaders to deliver the news. They are the Party's
spokesmen now. General Stanley McChrystal is among them. McChrystal,
in case you don't remember, is the strategic genius who can take credit
(if you can call it that) for running the longest losing war in American
history, the one in Afghanistan, the war that's still going.*

Yesterday, McChrystal took a break from collecting fat corporate director's fees to note that, based on his extensive experience mismanaging America's foreign policy, Trump voters look an awful lot like terrorists— an awful lot. Quote: "…I did see a similar dynamic of the evolution of al-Qaeda in Iraq," McChrystal said, "where a whole generation of angry Arab youth with very poor prospects followed a very powerful leader who promised to take them back in time to a better place, and he led them to embrace an ideology that justified their violence. This is now happening in America."

Al-Qaeda in America. Thanks, Stan. Sometime when you can manage to spare a moment from getting rich from your failures in America's decline, we'd love to know exactly what did happen in Afghanistan; what went wrong there? When you have time.

Until then though, Andy McCabe would like to put a finer point on the matter. You remember Andy McCabe. He's the former high-level FBI official who was canned for lying and corruption—a model federal employee. So when Andy McCabe speaks, you can hear the moral authority in his voice, gravelly and resonant, like cigarette smoke. You're going to want to listen carefully to what Andy McCabe has to say.

According to Andy McCabe's considered judgment, Donald Trump's voters are very much like ISIS. Listen to this: [Plays video clip]

[McCabe]: "When we looked at those Americans who travelled to Syria for the purpose of joining the Islamic State, when you put all those faces and names down in one place, you had doctors, lawyers…some people are very vulnerable to and drawn into that core lie of any extremist movement, and that is exactly what we are seeing now with this particular group of Trump supporters." [End video clip]

[Tucker]: Wait. American national security official Andy McCabe is telling us they're like ISIS—Islamic State in Syria? Aren't those the wild-eyed lunatics who beheaded journalists and set all those people on fire and then videotaped themselves doing it? Wow! That's terrifying!

That's right, Mr. and Mrs. America—what we didn't tell you before was that ISIS *was for Donald Trump. That's why they were murdering so many people. They were the Syrian branch of* MAGA. *You may have heard it was some kind of Islamic thing—c'mon! That's racist. It was Donald Trump all along. Now, those people are in this country; in Dallas, in Sarasota, in Newport Beach—everywhere! They're hiding in plain sight! God knows what they will do next.*

Actually, we do know! Another 9/11. That's what [these Trump supporters] are planning. And that's why we need a new 9/11 commission to root them out. But, thankfully, commander Pelosi is planning one right now—watch! [Plays multiple video clips]

[Speaker Nancy Pelosi (D-CA)]: "There is a strong interest in the Congress in a 9/11-type commission."

[CNN guest]: "…deep look at a 9/11-style commission to get to all of what happened."

[Wolf Blitzer]: "Yeah, they need a 9/11-type commission of inquiry."

[Andy McCabe]: "Along the lines of a 9/11 commission."

[Senator Richard Blumenthal (D-CT)]: "A 9/11-type commission."

[CNN guest]: "And hopefully an independent 9/11-style commission will look at…"

[Jim Comey]: "I think this is a big enough threat, an attack on the center of our democracy, that it's going to need a look that spans branches of government, something closer to a 9/11 commission." [End video clips]

[Tucker]: Well, I think we know they're on the same email chain.

But that doesn't change the substance of what they just told you. Did you hear Jim Comey (another noted moral authority)? What Jim Comey told you is that what happened in Washington on January 6th—the Chewbacca guy stumbling around the House floor, and all of it—that was this generation's 9/11. And, in fact, the magnitude of that atrocity begs for a better name. So, from now on, we are going to call it "one-six" (1/6). And that day will live in infamy for all time. Your grandchildren will get the day off from school every January 6th in remembrance of the horror that took place. In fact, here's a better idea, let's call it "Insurrection Day," because, honestly, that's what it was. [Plays multiple video clips]

[Rep. Adam Schiff (D-CA)]: "The President incited an insurrection against Congress to prevent the peaceful transition of power."

[Rep. Cedric Richmond (D-LA)]: "And then, he sat back and watched the insurrection."

[Rep. Haley Stevens (D-MI)]: "Insurrection! A violent mob!"

[Rep. Cori Bush (D-MO)]: "A white supremacist president who incited a white supremacist insurrection."

[Rep. Ilhan Omar (D-MN)]: "...an insurrection against our government."

[Rep. Hakeem Jeffries (D-NY)]: "The violent attack on the US capitol was an act of insurrection."

[Speaker Pelosi]: "...to insurrection that violated the sanctity of the people's Capitol.

[Rep. Jim McGovern (D-MA)]: "This was not a protest! This was an insurrection!" [End video clips]

[Tucker]: Bruce Willis in "Insurrection Day!"

But it's not a joke. According to the Honorable Jim McGovern—and everyone else you saw on the screen—this was not a protest! How dare you call it that! This was an insurrection!...

But you should also know, by the way, for frame of reference, what an insurrection is not. For example, yesterday, 28 people arrested at a violent protest in New York (not on behalf of Donald Trump). Those people attacked police officers. A bunch of them went to jail. But know this: Were they insurrecting at the time?

No, they weren't.

How do we know they weren't?

Because they weren't racists. Only racists can insurrect. Listen carefully to congresswoman Ayanna Pressley explain: [Plays video clip]

[Rep. Ayanna Pressley (D-MA)]: "The threat of white supremacy looms large, and it is tragic that it took this insurrection and this attempt to interrupt the peaceful transfer of power, and moreover, injury and loss of life, for many to appreciate just how formidable the threat of white supremacy is." [End video clip]

[Tucker]: This is a tough one.

So, what do you do with insurrectionists like that? Insurrectionists who are also white supremacists (as they always are), but not—and here's the tricky part—in some cases, even white? So you have nonwhite white supremacists who insurrect! That's very tough. How do you handle that? Simple force doesn't always work—these are hard cases.

You need to reeducate people like that, possibly in camps—"reeducation camps," if you will. You must deprogram them for the safety of the rest of us.

Thankfully, Sandy Cortez has been thinking about this for quite some time. ... [she] knows exactly what to do now. [Plays video clip]

[Rep. Alexandria Ocasio-Cortez (D-NY)]: "We had a program addressing white supremacists, uh, that...we had programs, federal programs, that went towards funding organizations like these that de-radicalized people, and President Trump pulled the plug on federal funding for some of these programs. And so, one thing that we know is that we have to get that funding right back up, and we probably need to double, triple, quadruple, um, or increase funding for these de-radicalization programs." [End video clip]

[Tucker]: So, you listen to that—and all of this—and you realize the totalitarian instinct is always the same—always. Only the names of the dictators change. First, you strip people of their right to speak out loud—honestly. Then you prevent them from defending themselves and their families. And then, because you now can, you force them at gunpoint to read your catechism, to accept your orthodoxy. You wonder if Sandy

Cortez plans to make Trump voters sign written statements affirming they have been deprogrammed. Of course. That's always part of the process.

The scary thing is, that's where we're heading. Sandy Cortez and her friends are no longer a fringe element within the Democratic Party. Joe Biden ran as a moderate. People voted for him because they thought he was. But Joe Biden's victory was really a victory for Sandy Cortez and that part of the Democratic Party. They are closer now than they've ever been to taking control.

The reason for that is very simple.

There is a massive power vacuum at the center of this incoming administration, the one that takes power tomorrow. Joe Biden is fading. That is not a personal attack on Joe Biden, it is real. Joe Biden is not capable of running the government or pushing back against the radicals in his party. The people around Joe Biden know this very well, and that includes people very close to him, including his relatives. People who love Joe Biden were upset when he ran for President. They know he can't do the job and they are very worried about what happens next. That is not speculation; they have said so out loud, and no honest person in Joe Biden's orbit will deny this.

So, the question is, who will fill the power vacuum within the Biden administration?

There are still—and we're being as honest as we can be—there are still reasonable people within the Democratic Party. There are people who have a stake in this country—people who don't want to destroy it. And now is the time for those people, the reasonable people in the democratic party, to step up forcefully and call off the war their party is planning on millions of fellow Americans. And it is war they're planning.

A 9/11 commission
Blanket censorship
Mass arrests
Deprogramming

These are not subtle indicators. These are fire alarms, and everyone can see them! No one seems to care at the moment. In the last week, CNN and The Washington Post have called for Fox News to be shut down by force. Why?

Because they don't like our views, so we should be banned.

In a normal country, reasonable people, including other journalists, might stand up and say: "Hold on! Censorship is wrong. Censorship only serves the powerful." But they've said nothing because they agree.

Meanwhile, our elected officials become openly authoritarian and no one pushes back. D.C. Mayor Muriel Bowser said she would like the National Guard to place crew-served machine guns—belt-fed .50-cals—around the city. This, in addition to 26,000 federal troops—more than Abraham Lincoln had defending the Capitol in 1864. But we need those, she said, because Trump voters are that dangerous.

What did the massive-infrastructure, professional Libertarians in Washington say to this? Nothing. They were silent.

What did Mitch McConnell say—the Republican leader of the Senate? Nothing. He was too busy attacking Trump voters for being the real threat.

Other members of Congress, on the other side, just tore off their mask completely and launched into open race-hate on television. That's not an exaggeration. We wish it was. Here's Congressman Jamaal Bowman explaining the real problem with this country is white people. They're the threat to progress. [Plays video clip]

[Rep. Jamaal Bowman (D-NY)]: "But this is a chance for all of us in Congress to sort of begin at a new baseline, and stop spreading the myth of American exceptionalism, and accept the fact that this is exactly who we are, this is exactly who we've been throughout our country's history. Whenever there's social progress, there's white backlash." [End video clip]

[Tucker]: The story here is not that one member of Congress said this on television. The story is that many members of Congress, and members of our media, say this on television every single day; attack huge groups of

Americans on the basis of their skin color, and nobody says anything—nobody pushes back, as if there are no consequences to talking that way.

But there are.

How long can people keep talking like that, and keep acting like this, irresponsibly, crazily, before something breaks? Before one of those 74 million haunted-terrorist-Trotskyite-wreckers we keep hearing about, becomes so overwrought and paranoid from watching demagogues like Jamaal Bowman attack him on MSNBC, that he does something truly awful that can't be taken back, and then the cycle accelerates radically, and an awful lot of people get hurt?

That's where this is going. Everyone knows it. That's where this will go until and unless someone responsible within the Democratic Party appears and puts a stop to it, and soon!

It's time for the victors to accept their victory, to forgive the team they beat, and to move on. You won! Be happy! Now improve the country you inherited. [End transcript]

The transcript of Tucker's show should be sobering for all Americans. Yet, many American's naively dismiss the Left's rhetoric as benign. The examples Tucker draws upon demonstrate that such rhetoric is far from benign. Culturally, we are divided. The Marxist impulse fuels Leftist rhetoric, demonizing entire groups of people based on who they are, not anything they have done. As we saw in Chapter 6, progressive Social Justice servicemember activists parrot this rhetoric and even threaten their fellow American citizens.

I do, however, disagree with one of Tucker's concluding points. He asserts: "that's where this is going—everyone knows it."

On the contrary, not everyone does know it. And the kind of violence Tucker envisions often takes nations by surprise. We will discuss that later in this chapter.

Since the evening show of January 19, Tucker has begun drawing attention to the "woke" US military services, alleging they are becoming more concerned with Diversity and Inclusion than with winning wars, and pointing out how they are more focused on dress and grooming standards than they should be. In a defensive move indicating the sting of Tucker's remarks, active-duty servicemembers—even senior leaders—have taken to social media to attack him. Pentagon spokesperson John Kirby has also spoken out against Tucker.

Tucker's warnings are important, and his show is watched by far more people than will likely ever read this book. But perhaps you have read this far because you are supposed to read this warning, too. This book has been written for you.

Once Respected, Now Despised

AT THE BEGINNING OF CHAPTER 3, we looked briefly at the Chinese Cultural Revolution of 1966-67. We revisit that now and begin with the story of one General Luo. Mao's revolution serves as a reminder that ideas have consequences—that terrible ideas have terrible consequences.

As Chinese comrades in the struggle sought to expose "hidden enemies" of the revolution, not even the country's once-respected military leaders were exempt from targeted attacks. Once Marxism's party line was firmly established in the country, senior military leaders were expected to adopt it. If they did not, they too became enemies of the revolution. Once considered the nation's protectors, they were now merely dissidents.

The "struggle rallies" Fan Shen describes in his memoir became opportunities to parade and humiliate "capitalists and their running dogs."[286] Revolutionaries, of course, loosely defined those running dogs as anyone they themselves perceived as an opponent to the revolutionary cause—defenders of old society.

The first mass rally Shen attended was in late June, after the temperatures had risen exponentially throughout Beijing making such gatherings possible. Shen explains that a "gigantic open stage" was constructed on the soccer field specifically for such events, and this first one was "against General Luo, the former Chief of Staff of the People's Liberation Army, who the Red Guards said was a hidden traitor."[287] As usual, before the rally began, Shen and his friends worked their way through the legs of adults and found a perfect spot directly in front of the stage. These young boys sat amidst a sea of red—"red flags, red armbands, red banners with slogans"—and they were very excited and eager to do their part to "fight the enemy" who had been hiding in the army for so many years.[288]

"When the rally started in the early evening," Shen explains, "the general was brought onto the stage by two Red Guards amid a deafening roar of revolutionary slogans. He wore white casts on both his legs and could not stand on his own."[289] According to a nearby member of the Red Guard, he had jumped from a second-floor window in what was either a real or pretended suicide attempt. The general sat planted in a chair on the stage in front of his roaring audience. As the guards released their grip on the man and turned their backs, the old man collapsed and slumped to the ground. Shen describes the general's appearance: "In the sharp bluish floodlight, his face had turned ghastly white, like a piece of tofu."

"He's playing dead!" someone shouted.

"Pull him up! Pull him up!" others shouted.

"Pretending to be dead won't save your skin!" one of the Red Guards yelled at his white, lifeless face.

Shen's account continues:

A soldier with a red armband strutted over and splashed a glass of cold water on the ashen face on the ground, but the general barely moved. The soldier bent down and pulled the general's head up by the hair. We clapped our hands and laughed at the distorted, ugly face. The old man moaned and his jaws flapped mechanically as if he were drowning, gasping for air.

"He knows how to put on a show," our informant said to us and we all laughed.

"Don't try to fool us," I shouted to the old man. "Stand up and face the people!"

The soldier propped him up on the chair again. From where we stood, we could almost touch the general's blanched face. His face was so haunting in its pallor that many nights after the rally I could still vividly see the sunken eye sockets, the bluish lips, the chalky skin wrapped around a skeleton, the sweat-soaked dusty green uniform, the half-torn insignia, the trembling hands. Of course, as I gazed at the ghastly figure, I felt no pity.

Now that the target of the rally had been stabilized, the meeting began. As with all such rallies, it began with thunderous slogans bellowed from loudspeakers. Like a row of gigantic black toads, the loudspeakers formed a semicircle around the edge of the stage, barely three yards from our faces. The sound from them was so powerful that I could feel each syllable strike my face.

"CONFESSION OR DEATH!"

"LONG LIVE THE RED TERROR!"

"LONG LIVE THE GREAT CULTURAL REVOLUTION!"

We raised our fists and shouted with the loudspeakers. The shouting served its purpose. It got our blood boiling and we got more and more angry at the enemy sitting before us. One after another, people read indictment papers and we shouted more slogans after each one. We were halfway through the rally when the old general against slipped off the chair and slumped to the ground.

"He's playing dead again! My friends and I shouted. "Get him up! Get him up!"

A soldier walked over and tried to pull him back onto the chair. He then frowned and checked the old general's pulse. "He's dead!" he shouted to the people in front of the stage. "He's really dead!"

We did not believe him. Several people went on stage and checked again. But it was true. The man was dead—probably from a heart attack.

We did not feel sorry for him, though. Revolutionaries, as we were taught since childhood, should feel no mercy for enemies. In fact, we became angrier at him for dying so soon. The rally went on with even greater fervor for another hour, and I, along with all the Red Guards, shouted slogans at the dead body on the chair, denouncing the general's treacherous final act of escaping the revolution prematurely. It was the first time that I saw a dead man, *but I did not feel the terror of death, for the fervor of the revolutionary fire around me had temporarily removed the possibility of fear.*[290] (Italics added)

The mayor of Beijing and his wife were the targets of the second mass rally. In what revolutionaries deemed comedic, the mayor and his wife were dressed in clothes that would humiliate them—for her, the clothes were too tight and cut up the side so as to "expose her red underwear," and to "see her plump white thighs."[291] During the rally, half of her head was shaved by the Red Guard, and she was given high-heeled shoes that were too small, and made to "walk about the stage like a prostitute."[292] Because the couple was submissive, kneeling and knocking their skulls on the stage loudly when told to do so, they survived the ordeal "without much bodily harm."[293]

To resist the demands of the Red Guard, on the other hand, was to risk life and limb, and the revolutionaries were far from finished with military leadership, some of whom, trained to be tough and unyielding, were sure to refuse the unjust demands of the angry mob.

During the third massive rally, another general officer was their target—General Hei, Deputy Commander of the People's Liberation Army (PLA). The rally revolving around General Hei did not culminate in the jocular way the previous rally had with the mayor and his wife. Rather than submit, the courageous general resisted the mob's demands. Shen remembers:

This was a much more serious rally and had none of the comic atmosphere of the previous rally. From the very beginning of the rally, we found that we were faced with a hardcore enemy who refused to submit to the will of the revolutionary people. As soon as he was brought on stage, General Hei refused to bow down before the people. He was a large and powerful man and when two Red Guards tried to press his head down, he struggled fiercely to keep his head up. Finally, amid deafening slogans from the loudspeakers, an angry Red Guard member leaped onto the stage, slapped the general, tore off his red insignia, and stripped him to his underwear. We all cheered and applauded.

"That's right!" [one] shouted. "Teach him a lesson!"

"DEATH TO THOSE WHO REFUSE TO BOW DOWN BEFORE THE PEOPLE!"

"DOWN WITH THE HARDENED ENEMY GENERAL HEI!"

The two announcers shouted angrily over the loudspeakers, and we all raised our fists and shouted with them. Blood dripped from the old man's mouth. The general was shocked by the blows and by the thunderous shouting of thousands of voices. He ceased to struggle and let his head be pressed down, but the people were not satisfied. "Give him an airplane ride!" someone shouted in the audience. "Yes, an airplane ride! An airplane ride!" we all shouted in chorus. Following popular demand, the three Red Guards on stage twisted his arms back like the wings of an airplane and forced him to bend over until his face almost touched the ground. In just a few minutes, his face became a giant purple raspberry, and a long strand of saliva extended from his mouth onto the stage floor. Despite the airplane ride, General Hei was tough and did not beg for mercy, and he got more for his stubbornness.

After the rally, he was paraded around the Big Courtyard in his underwear. A Red Guard tied a rope around his neck and led him around like a dog. We followed him all the way and prodded his side with sticks whenever he slowed down. *I felt no guilt at all* when I thrust my stick into the man's bruised legs and arms to get him going. I was a good revolutionary then.[294] (Italics added)

Several days after the mass rally where General Hei was victimized and humiliated, Shen recounts the first time he sensed that he was engaging in a cause that was unjust—something dark. It was when he saw his first bloody body that he began to experience the fear of the revolution's brutal force.

As he and his friends sat eating lunch in the public dining hall, they heard a commotion outside and saw people running in one direction with great interest. They threw down their chopsticks and ran outside to investigate. "What happened?" Shen asked, after flagging down a young boy who trailed a group of older boys. "A body, a dead man. Someone…jumped off…a building," stammered the boy, out of breath.

"Despite the crowd, there was not a sound to be heard," Shen remembers. "Everybody was still and was staring at a twisted lump lying motionless on the concrete. The man must have landed on his head, for it had half disappeared into his neck. Dark blood soaked his brown uniform. His hands were tied behind his back. Since he was facing down, I could see only the back of his head. His white hair, sticky with blood, stood up like the needles on the back of a porcupine."[295]

The young men inquired as to the identity of the dead man. "General Hei," answered a tall, skinny young man who did not bother to turn his face as he spoke. Shen remembered the old man's agonized demeanor when he was paraded in his underwear only a few days before. It was so recent that he could still remember how it felt when his stick struck the man's thigh.

For the first time, Shen was struck with emotion. He began to sense the evil of his pursuit. "No need to pity him," a soldier with a red armband said to break the spell of silence. "He was a hidden enemy of the revolution. This is what he deserved in the first place."[296]

As I read the tragic account of General Hei—as he is being slapped on stage and having the insignia torn from his uniform—one question I have is, where are his fellow PLA servicemembers? He was the Deputy Commander of the PLA. Where was his boss, the Commander of the PLA? How did PLA servicemembers become so divided that they refused to stand up for one another against these revolutionary thugs? The answer is found in the divisive rhetoric of Marxist ideology. It is found in the fact that some members of the PLA believed in the Marxist revolutionary cause. It is found in the fact that men became fearful and gave in to the demands of an angry mob.

In one respect, US military servicemembers are no different than members of the People's Liberation Army. Each is comprised of humans—humans who share a common nature. Because we share the same nature, what Marxist ideology does to the Chinese military servicemember it will do to the American. It will divide them, pit them against one another, and sow the seeds of distrust, resentment, and anger.

Fratricidal and Genocidal Warfare

The pitiless cruelty exhibited by Mao's revolutionaries—by Chinese citizens against their fellow citizens—requires ideology. It was true not only in Mao's China, but in Lenin's and Stalin's Soviet Union, in Hitler's Nazi Germany, in Pol Pot's Cambodia, and any time in history when the forces of fratricidal and genocidal wrath were unleashed in society. For those who have not already succumbed to its seductive provocation, it is easy to see the rapid acceptance of such an ideology occurring right now in our own country.

To be perfectly clear, the path we are on as a country leads to fratricidal and genocidal warfare. By *fratricidal warfare* is meant the killing of one's own kin—family members. It is to despise and destroy fathers, mothers, brothers, sisters, or neighbors and fellow countrymen who share family-like ties, but who have adopted incompatible causes. By *genocidal warfare* is meant the killing of people because of their race, religion, ethnicity, or other indelible group membership.[297] Whether it is called genocide, or politicide (killing people because of their political affiliation), or democide (any mass killing of civilians by a government or militia), killing-by-category "targets people for what they *are* rather than what they *do*."[298] Of all the varieties of violence and warfare, genocide stands apart as particularly brutal and difficult to comprehend. For someone to be filled with the kind of rage and visceral animosity that they can justify brutalizing and killing innocent groups of people, to include women, children, and the elderly, flouts the usual motives for war.[299]

Genocidal violence is vengefully offensive in nature. It is purposeful and premeditated. Whereas war seeks to coerce an enemy for the achievement of certain political aims, genocide seeks extermination. Its logic is a kind of emotionally induced illogic. Those possessed of the logic of genocide cannot be reasoned with. Its destructive sweep leaves the innocent to either flee, or to pick up arms in defense of themselves, their families, and property. As author Steven Pinker observes in his *New York Times* Bestselling *Better Angels of Our Nature*, Genocide also "shocks the imagination by the sheer number of its victims." He writes:

> Rummel, who was among the first historians to try to count them all, famously estimated that during the 20th

century 169 million people were killed by their governments. The number is, to be sure, a highball estimate, but most atrocitologists agree that in the 20th century more people were killed by democides than by wars. Matthew White, in a comprehensive overview of the published estimates, reckons that 81 million people were killed by democide and another 40 million by man-made famines (mostly Stalin and Mao), for a total of 121 million. Wars, in comparison, killed 37 million soldiers and 27 million civilians in battle, and another 18 million in the resulting famines, for a total of 82 million deaths.[300]

Remember, Marxist ideology dictates that the enemy that is the object of the revolution's aims is, at first, a domestic one (see Chapter 4). Thus, acceptance of the ideology destroys a country from within. It breaks society apart. It demonizes whole groups of people who are considered oppressors simply by virtue of the way they look, the beliefs they hold, the size of their income, or the language they choose to employ in their interactions with others. In reality, however, it is the neo-Marxist practitioners themselves that have become domestic enemies.

In disheartening irony, the politically correct, overly sensitive, racially charged, woke culture in which we live prevents peaceful citizens from properly publicly identifying real threats for what they are. More disheartening still, is that even some of the US military's leaders use positions of power to further the Marxist agenda, as we have seen. Thus wittingly, or not, servicemembers are complicit in the unmaking of the American military and the moral decline of the country. Perhaps this book might awaken those who have been unwitting participants in "the struggle."

Those of us in uniform should know better. Fortunately, many do.

Military servicemembers of all ranks are becoming just as polarized in their views as the rest of the country. In one sense, that is not surprising. After all, the present polarization is not merely political; disagreements, as we have seen, are not simply over partisan education, energy, or immigration policies, which most servicemembers gladly avoid. No, our disagreements go beyond policy.

As is expected whenever Marxist ideology takes root, our disagreements have become increasingly grounded in beliefs about *what America was, is, and should become.* Such polarization is therefore also cultural. The Marxist conquest is achieving precisely what it set out to accomplish—to fracture American society from within. Servicemembers who are determined to remain apolitical now discover that even their beliefs and values have been characterized as suspect by the increasingly radicalized Left, so long as their beliefs and values seem aligned with "old society." Once the Left became a welcome host to Marxist ideology, our disagreements ceased to be about what we once called "partisan politics." They are now about national identity—about America's founding philosophy, culture, and history.[301] If what is meant by "remaining apolitical" is *remaining silent* in the face of anti-American, genocidal rhetoric, then the time for remaining apolitical is over.

We must believe that such silence, however, *is not our obligation at all*—neither as military servicemembers nor as Americans. Defending the Constitution first of all means believing in it, not demonizing it or its authors. It means speaking in its defense.

In Thucydides' *History of the Peloponnesian War* (431-404 BC), one of the greatest classics of military theory and history ever written, we learn more about the ideological division of society that is both *the cause* and *result of* domestic conflict. Thucydides' explained "the *violent fanaticism* which came into play *once the struggle had broken out....*As the result of these revolutions, there was a general deterioration of character throughout the Greek world....Society had become *divided into two ideologically hostile camps*, and each side viewed the other with suspicion."[302] (Italics added)

The continued social and political polarization of Americans corresponds to the intensity of the ideological division between groups. The veiled civil war once described by Marx is "no longer over specific gains or losses but over conceptions of moral right and over the interpretation of history and human destiny."[303] Stathis Kalyvas, in his landmark study on civil wars, helps us conceptualize this polarization. It is the "sum of antagonisms between individuals belonging to a small number of groups that simultaneously display high internal homogeneity and high external heterogeneity."[304] Once polarization occurs, Kalyvas describes how natural it is for society to descend into violence:

> The intuition is that if a population is clustered around a small number of distant but equally large poles, it is likely to undergo violent conflict. A typical claim is that "civil wars are by their nature often more savage than international wars, and have a stronger ideological content. The two factors are certainly related"....*The underlining mechanism is dislike so intense as to cancel even fraternal ties, imagined or real. "Identity...is what gets the blood boiling*, what makes people do unspeakable things to their neighbors. It is the fuel used by agitators to set whole countries on fire."[305] (Italics added)

Once the blood gets boiling, the rapid onset of violence often takes societies by surprise. When the revolution *breaks out*, it is more like a natural phenomenon than the result of human action.[306] It appears almost "random," explains Kalyvas, "inexplicable, indelible, like a lightning bolt or wildfire."[307] A woman described her perception of the violence of the Spanish Civil War as "a sudden outburst erupting like a volcano."[308] A Guatemalan Indian recalled the violence his country experienced from 1980-1982 by saying "he and his neighbors fell victim to temporary madness."[309] Another described the violence at the beginning of the civil war in Lebanon: "It was as if Beirut had gone totally mad."[310] In yet another conflict, both Bosnian Muslims and Croats complained of "a kind of madness taking people over, and changing them unexpectedly."[311] "We always lived together and got along well; what is happening now has been created by something stronger than us."[312] Kalyvas explains that what researchers have found is that this madness, and the accompanying civil war, nearly always takes people by surprise:

> Survey research conducted in Yugoslavia during the mid-1990s found that only 7 percent of the respondents believed that the country would break up....Noel Malcolm (1998) summarizes these observations: "What comes across most strongly from [the] personal histories [of the Bosnian War] is the sense of bewilderment most people felt. The outbreak of the war took them by surprise, and the transformation of neighbors into enemies seemed to have no basis in their previous experience. Their favorite metaphor was that *a whirlwind had come out of nowhere and blew their lives apart.*"[313] (Italics added)

Averting the Wrath to Come

What is to be done about all of this? What is *our obligation* in the face of an ideology that suppresses thought, demands conformity, propounds distortions, and threatens to burn down society until it becomes a smoldering heap? Is it possible to avert the looming peril? To escape or flee the wrath to come?

The optimal way for the United States to curtail its destructive march is by committing to national repentance. But what is optimal is unlikely. "True, repentant political parties are," in

Solzhenitsyn's words, "about as frequently encountered in history as tiger-doves."[314] "Politicians of course can still repent—many of them do not lose their human qualities. But *parties* are obviously utterly inhuman formations, and the very object of their existence precludes repentance."[315]

As the kind of collective repentance required to avert crisis seems an untenable solution to our problems, the burden of repentance and proper being rests squarely upon the shoulders of individuals, families, and small groups or communities. Therefore, educate yourself and choose to be the kind of citizen that allows civil society to flourish. I have written this book with the hope that it will be an important part of that education.

If the nation remains divided and becomes increasingly polarized, however, then averting the wrath to come may not be possible, and Marxism's goal of conquest will indeed be realized in the very country Engels referred to as "the last Bourgeois Paradise on earth"—the United States. Engels predicted what the collapse of America would mean for the entire free world: it would be the "snapping of their mainstay." Averting the wrath to come is up to every one of us. While relative peace remains, be as salt to preserve society by helping teach others.

Our repentance consists of abandoning the web of deception and the fog of lies in which we all labor. Such a challenge is not impossible, but it requires seeking for and turning to truth. It requires us to abandon arrogance and to become humble. If you are a Christian, it means turning away from sin and turning to Christ. If you are a Jew, it means turning and facing the God of Abraham, Isaac, and Jacob. Whatever your faith, religion, or spiritual ambition, it means turning from evil and pursuing good. For the religious and nonreligious alike, repentance also consists in Americans believing in America—in its fundamental goodness. It means believing in and adopting America's founding principles as our best hope as a country of healing and unifying, regardless of religion, creed, politics, or race.

You and I both have an important role to play as events unfold and as we labor within our own unique spheres of influence. Whether you are a parent, student, teacher, uniformed servicemember, elected official, business owner, stay-at-home parent, attorney, or radio talk show host—act well thy part. While I cannot pretend to understand the ways in which each person is postured to act, I hope that what follows proves beneficial.

Avoid anger and violence. Neither be overcome by nor fuel the anger that is advanced on social media. Stand for what is right but do not give others reason to be angry with you. Patiently persuade them in thoughtful dialogue, while remaining content with the idea that others believe differently than you. Do not seek out or get wrapped up in violence if and when it ensues. Violence will not solve the problems we face, but only compound them. Aside from your obligation to protect yourself, your family, and your property, bringing violence against others will only accelerate the Marxist revolutionary agenda.

Be courageous. You live in a season of human history that demands great courage. Be grateful for the opportunity that is before you and do not shrink from your obligations. Do not be a cowardly summer soldier or sunshine patriot. As you courageously stand for what is right, accept the consequences. As others observe your courage, they will learn courage. They will seek to emulate it.

Get educated. Learn about American history from the best books. By doing this, you will come to appreciate the greatness of America's founding ideas and ideals, the timelessness of the American philosophy found in the Declaration of Independence, the wisdom and beauty of our limited form of government as codified in the Constitution, and the inalienability of your natural rights as a US citizen as further enumerated in the Bill of Rights. If you are not sure where to begin, consult the short, recommended reading list at the end of this book.

Speak up. And when you speak up, speak the truth. You have a voice for a reason. Think and reason earnestly, understand thoroughly, and communicate judiciously with others in both private and public. Do not remain silent. In your day, at this time, given what we face, silence is acquiescence to the Marxist revolution.

Live not by lies. This was Solzhenitsyn's advice to the Russian people on the eve of his exile to the West. Follow it. He speaks from experience. This very mentality is the reason he was no longer welcome in the communist Soviet Union. Following his advice requires you to seek to understand the truth. Again, if you are not sure where to begin, start by rejecting the Marxist-rooted tenets of critical race theory and identity politics (see Chapter 5). Help others see that lies and stereotypes based on sex, race, and other demographics only further divide our country.

Pay attention. If you are a parent, know what the public education system is teaching your children. Own the responsibility of your child's education. As a citizen, know what is happening in your own home, in your workplace, in your community, in your country, and in the world.

Finally, if you wear the uniform of your country, do your job well. Learn to perform your unique mission with competence and technical expertise. The American people expect that of you.

I am confident that a great number of you already do that exceptionally well. I will likewise always strive to do the same. For example, my unit's obligation is to protect the Nation and our allies by providing timely missile warning around the clock. That remains true in peace time and war, and it is a service owed to the American people regardless of their domestic political disputes.

Faithfully accomplishing that mission is one way I honor my oath to support and defend the Constitution.

But in addition to doing your mission, you have important choices to make about how you will conduct yourself in and out of uniform. To the best of your ability, strive to remain apolitical in your speech in the current hyper-politicized environment. This means that partisan policy discussions fall outside of your sphere of activity. Allow the politician and the civilian citizen to be concerned with those things. That said, as an individual, you must:

Never be ashamed of your own beliefs—you are entitled to them.

Never forget that in America your right to speak freely is protected by Constitutional law—the supreme law of the land that you have sworn an oath to defend.

Never be ashamed to *believe* in the fundamental goodness of your country and the greatness of its ideals, or to *speak* in its defense.

Never use your position of authority to unduly propound partisan political views. To do so is to undermine good order and discipline.

Finally, our military services and servicemembers must remain patriotic. The US military must not facilitate the country's polarization. Instead, it should serve as one of the country's last institutional opportunities for the preservation of unity. Collectively, we must:

Never alienate or discriminate against people based on race, creed, color, sex, religion, ethnicity, national origin, or political views—it is against the law and it is wrong. This includes alienating or discriminating against conservatives, whites, cisgenders, heterosexuals, Jews, Christians, masculine men, feminine women, and any and every other identity group or affiliation that is constantly under rhetorical attack by postmodernists, neo-Marxists, cancel culturists, woke supremacists, and vindictive Social Justice activists.

Never insist that we live in and serve at the behest of a white supremacist country. If the services facilitate the spread of such lies, they will face retention problems on both sides of the political isle that will be extremely difficult to recover from.

Never force equality of outcomes or insist upon fulfilling race- and gender-based quotas as a substitution for our long-standing merit-based system.[316] If we do, we will lose our lethality.

AFTERWORD

I WAS NEVER INTERESTED in authoring a book—I'm still not.

Beginning in late-November 2020, the idea of writing this book settled upon me, like a bolt out of the blue. I couldn't shake the thought, and, not long thereafter, it weighed heavily upon me. The weight of that burden has remained with me as a constant reminder to finish the work.

I began writing in what small pockets of time I could find outside of my full-time job as a commander, a job I take very seriously and one that demands much of my time and attention. As one can imagine, writing a book in one's free time is less than ideal, though I know that others have done so before me. I've done it to be true to myself, to fulfill the obligation that was resting with me, and to honor the oath I have taken to defend the Constitution of the United States.

From the moment I began writing in the first week of December until today, it seemed that the material that should be covered in the book was constantly unfolded to my mind. And so, for four months I have labored daily to produce *Irresistible Revolution*. I trust it is a unique and beneficial contribution.

As acknowledged in the Introduction, it was more important to me that the book be published now than that I spend more time getting its contents and arguments perfectly cleaned up so as to ensure I might not unwittingly injure my own pride or image. That matters little to me. Therefore, I submit the work to the reader admitting that it surely contains errors and deficiencies that will only be made more fully known to me with time. Maybe I will consider improving upon the work at a later date, but, for now, I gladly finish writing. Undoubtedly, many conversations will follow.

Earlier this year, I met a friend for lunch, another officer, and we were discussing this book project and everything that was happening in the country. Offering encouragement for the book, he said: "At the end of the day, people want to fight for what's right."

I believe he is right. I believe that most of our uniformed servicemembers and many Americans believe in the fundamental goodness of our great country and want to preserve it. But fighting for what is right means first understanding the truth about what is happening. Only then, perhaps, will many more people act courageously in defense of their liberties and take a stand against a Marxist revolution that has become nearly irresistible.

I hope this book is a tool in the hands of those who choose to stand for what is right.

Matthew Lohmeier
April 6, 2021

SUGGESTED READING

My own writing has relied heavily upon the contributions of many others whose works are referenced later in the endnotes. As promised in the book, I am providing a suggested reading list for those who may not know where to begin their own education regarding some of the important topics we have covered. I hope this list proves a helpful starting place.

The list that follows is broken out by topic, is relatively short so as not to be burdensome, and, of course, reflects my own idiosyncrasies. While some are more modern works, others are classics that will be recognized and widely read by serious students of these topics. Though the works that follow have shaped my own understanding in important ways, they are but a small sampling of a vast library of valuable contributions from many others that might aide you in your own education. I have indicated with an asterisk what I think would be a great starting place in each category.

American History, Philosophy & Government:

Arnn, Larry P., Carol Swain et al. *The 1776 Commission Report*. Independently Published, 2021.

Hamilton, Alexander, John Jay, and James Madison. *The Federalist Papers*. USA: Simon & Brown, 2010.

Johnson, Paul. *A History of the American People*. New York: HarperCollins, 1997.

Levin, Mark. *Ameritopia: The Unmaking of America*. New York: Threshold Editions, 2012.

Levin, Mark. *Liberty and Tyranny: A Conservative Manifesto.* New York: Threshold Editions, 2009.

Levin, Mark. *Rediscovering Americanism: And the Tyranny of Progressivism.* New York: Threshold Editions, 2017.

Locke, John. *The Second Treatise of Government.* New York: Macmillan Publishing Company, 1952. First published 1690.

*McClay, Wilfred M. *Land of Hope: An Invitation to the Great American Story.* New York: Encounter Books, 2019.

Reilly, Robert R. *America on Trial: A Defense of the Founding.* San Francisco: Ignatius Press, 2020.

The Hillsdale College Politics Department, ed. *The U.S. Constitution: A Reader.* Hillsdale, Mi: Hillsdale College Press, 2013.

The Declaration of Independence

The Constitution of the United States

Marxism & Communism:

Marx, Karl, and Friedrich Engels. *The Communist Manifesto.* New York: Penguin Books, 2002. First published 1848.

Ngo, Andy. *Unmasked: Inside Antifa's Radical Plan to Destroy Democracy.* New York: Hachette Book Group, 2021.

Shen, Fan. *Gang of One: Memoirs of a Red Guard.* Lincoln: University of Nebraska Press, 2004.

Solzhenitsyn, Alexander, Mikhail Agursky et al. *From Under the Rubble.* Boston: Little, Brown and Company, 1975.

*The Epoch Times. *How the Specter of Communism is Ruling our World.* 3 vols. New York: The Epoch Times, 2020.

Race Studies & Diversity:

Leonard, Thomas C. *Illiberal Reformers: Race, Eugenics & American Economics in the Progressive Era.* Princeton, NJ: Princeton University Press, 2016.

Mac Donald, Heather. *The Diversity Delusion: How Race and Gender Pandering Corrupt the University and Undermine Our Culture.* New York: St. Martin's Publishing Group, 2018.

Sandefur, Timothy. *Frederick Douglass: Self-made Man.* Washington, DC: CATO Institute, 2018.

*Steele, Shelby. *White Guilt: How Blacks and Whites Together Destroyed the Promise of the Civil Rights Era.* New York: HarperCollins, 2006.

Steele, Shelby. *The Content of Our Character: A New Vision of Race in America.* New York: HarperCollins, 1990.

Sowell, Thomas. *Discrimination and Disparities.* New York: Basic Books, 2018.

Postmodernism, Critical Theories, Ideology, Totalitarianism, Other:

Arendt, Hannah. *The Origins of Totalitarianism.* New York: Houghton Mifflin, 1968. First published 1951.

Butcher, Jonathan, and Mike Gonzales. "Critical Race Theory, the New Intolerance, and its Grip on America." Washington, DC: The Heritage Foundation, 2021.

Gonzalez, Mike. *The Plot to Change America: How Identity Politics is Dividing the Land of the Free.* New York: Encounter Books, 2020.

Hayek, F.A. *The Road to Serfdom.* Chicago: The University of Chicago Press, 1994. First published 1944.

Hicks, Stephen R.C. *Explaining Postmodernism: Skepticism and Socialism from Rousseau to Foucault.* Aberdeen City, UK: Ockham's Razor Publishing, 2011.

Murray, Douglas. *The Madness of Crowds: Gender, Race and Identity.* London: Bloomsbury Continuum, 2019.

Peterson, Jordan B. *Maps of Meaning: The Architecture of Belief.* New York: Routledge, 1999.

*Pluckrose, Helen, and James Lindsay. *Cynical Theories: How Activist Scholarship Made Everything about Race, Gender, and Identity—and Why This Harms Everybody.* Durham, NC: Pitchstone Publishing, 2020.

Saad, Gad. *The Parasitic Mind: How Infectious Ideas are Killing Common Sense.* Washington, DC: Regnery Publishing, 2020.

ACKNOWLEDGEMENTS

I owe a debt of gratitude to many trustworthy friends, both old and new, who have helped me along the way. Thank you to Aaron, Denver, Jack, Janson, Jim, John, Kay, Ron, Taylor, my wife Sara, and my mom and dad for reading, critiquing, and providing edits to and suggestions for the text, as well as offering other input, guidance, and support during the writing process.

I am encouraged by and grateful for the ongoing efforts of nascent grassroots groups such as STARRS (Stand Together Against Racism and Radicalism in the Services) who partner with our military armed services to promote unity over division, and help educate military leaders, servicemembers, and the American people of the dangers of neo-Marxist and critical race theory ideologies. Thank you for working tirelessly to ensure our military services remain free of undue political influence, and thank you for your support.

Thank you to attorneys Jeff McFadden, Michael T. Rose, and Joe Traficanti for providing expert legal counsel and for spending extra time with certain sensitive sections of the book. Your advice was critical and has allowed me to publish my work with added confidence.

I am indebted to Kevin Merrell for his outstanding and expeditious work on the internal design of the book, to David Christenson for graciously lending his talent in the creation of the cover art, and to Reed Larsen for offering his expertise in marketing.

Last, and once again, thank you to my wife and also to my children for bearing with me through this exceptionally busy time. Sara, you have brought added balance and wisdom to the text that I was incapable of on my own. I am grateful for your love and support.

ENDNOTES

Notes to Chapter 1

1. With the common reader in mind, I selectively abandon the nuance of various academic terms such as "neo-Marxism" when referring to new or contemporary Marxist thought.

2. Department of Defense Instruction (DoDI) 1325.06, *Handling Dissident and Protest Activities Among Members of the Armed Forces*, November 27, 2009, 9.

3. The February 5, 2021 memorandum can be found online at https://media.defense.gov/2021/Feb/05/2002577485/-1/-1/0/STAND-DOWN-TO-ADDRESS-EXTREMISM-IN-THE-RANKS.PDF.

4. George Orwell, *1984* (New York, NY: Houghton Mifflin Harcourt, 1949), 19.

5. Ibid., 33.

6. Igor Shafarevich, "Separation or Reconciliation?—The Nationalities Question in the USSR," in Alexander Solzhenitsyn, *From Under the Rubble* (Boston, MA: Little, Brown and Company, 1975), 94-95.

7. Ibid.

8. Zoe Greenberg, "Boston Globe launches 'Fresh Start' initiative: People can apply to have past coverage about them reviewed," *The Boston Globe*, January 22, 2021, accessed on February 25, 2021, https://www.bostonglobe.com/2021/01/22/metro/boston-globe-launches-fresh-start-initiative-people-can-apply-update-or-anonymize-coverage-them-thats-online/.

9. Ibid.

10. Elliot Kaufman, "The '1619 Project' Gets Schooled," *Wall Street Journal*, December 16, 2019, accessed on February 25, 2021, https://www.wsj.com/articles/the-1619-project-gets-schooled-11576540494.

11. Nikole Hannah-Jones, et al., "The 1619 Project," *The New York Times Magazine*, August 18, 2019, https://pulitzercenter.org/sites/default/files/full_issue_of_the_1619_project.pdf.

12. Ibid., 17.

13. Gregg Ivers, "The Constitutional Vision of Martin Luther King, Jr.," *Expert Forum*, January 14, 2018, accessed on February 25, 2021, https://www.acslaw.org/expertforum/the-constitutional-vision-of-martin-luther-king-jr/.

14. Hannah-Jones, "The 1619 Project," 26.

15. Ibid.

16. Ibid., 54.

17. Ibid., 30.

18. Ibid., 70.

19. Ibid., 48.

20. Adam Serwer, "The Fight Over the 1619 Project Is Not About the Facts," *The Atlantic*, December 23, 2019, accessed on February 25, 2021, https://www.theatlantic.com/ideas/archive/2019/12/historians-clash-1619-project/604093/.

21. Wilfred McClay, *Land of Hope: An Invitation to the Great American Story* (New York, NY: Encounter Books, 2019), 140.

22. Ibid., 142.

23. Peter W. Wood, *1620: A Critical Response to the 1619 Project* (New York, NY: Encounter Books, 2020), 5-6.

24. Ibid.

25. Ibid., 39.

26. Kaufman, "The '1619 Project' Gets Schooled."

27. Howard Zinn, *A People's History of the United States* (New York, NY: HarperCollins, 2015), 631.

28. Ibid., 640.

29. Ibid., 635.

30. Eric London and David North, "Nikole Hannah-Jones, race theory and the Holocaust," *WSWS*, November 26, 2019, accessed on February 25, 2021, https://www.wsws.org/en/articles/2019/11/26/1619-n26.html.

31. Ibid.

32. Jordan Davidson, "In Racist Screed, NYT's 1619 Project Founder Calls 'White Race' 'Barbaric Devils,' 'Bloodsuckers,' Columbus 'No Different Than Hitler," *The Federalist*, June 25, 2020, accessed on February 25, 2021, https://thefederalist.com/2020/06/25/in-racist-screed-nyts-1619-project-founder-calls-white-race-barbaric-devils-bloodsuckers-no-different-than-hitler/.

33. Wood, *1620*, 40.

34. Shafarevich, "Separation or Reconciliation?" 96.

35. "Establishing the President's Advisory 1776 Commission," Executive Order 13958 of November 2, 2020, accessed on February 26, 2021, https://www.federalregister.gov/documents/2020/11/05/2020-24793/establishing-the-presidents-advisory-1776-commission, 1.

36. Ibid.

37. Emiene Wright, "Biden Moves to 'Defeat the Lies,' Starting with Dismantling the 1776 Commission," *Courier Newsroom*, January 21, 2021, accessed on March 4, 2021, https://couriernewsroom.com/2021/01/21/biden-dismantles-1776-commission/.

38. Lynn Sweet, "Biden's first actions to eliminate systemic racism: So long to Trump's 1776 Commission," *Chicago Sun Times*, January 26, 2021, accessed on March 4, 2021, https://chicago.suntimes.com/columnists/2021/1/26/22251548/joe-biden-susan-rice-executive-orders-systemic-racism-trump-1776-commission-private-prisons-aapi.

39. Brittany Bernstein, "Biden Signs Executive Order Disbanding 1776 Commission," *National Review*, January 20, 2021, accessed on March 4, 2021, https://www.nationalreview.com/news/biden-signs-executive-order-disbanding-1776-commission/; see also "Biden signs executive order to disband Trump's 1776 Commission," *KTLA5*, January 21, 2021, accessed on March 4, 2021, https://ktla.com/news/nationworld/biden-disbands-trumps-1776-commission-revokes-report-aimed-at-promoting-patriotic-education/.

40. Colleen Flaherty, "A Push for 'Patriotic Education,'" *Inside Higher Ed*, January 20, 2021, accessed on March 4, 2021, https://www.insidehighered.com/news/2021/01/20/historians-trump-administrations-report-us-history-belongs-trash.

41. Ibid.

42. Paul Blest, "Trump's 'Last Great Lie' is the 1776 Report That Whitewashes Slavery," *Vice News*, January 19, 2021, accessed on March 4, 2021, https://www.vice.com/en/article/88akab/trumps-last-big-lie-the-1776-report-that-whitewashes-slavery.

43. Kevin Mahnken, "On His First Day in White House, Biden Dissolves Trump's 1776 Commission on U.S. History," The 74 Million, January 20, 2021, accessed on March 4, 2021, https://www.the74million.org/on-his-first-day-in-white-house-biden-dissolves-trumps-1776-commission-on-u-s-history/.

44. Caroline Kelly, "Biden rescinds 1776 commission via executive order," *CNN*, January 21, 2021, accessed on March 4, 2021, https://www.cnn.com/2021/01/20/politics/biden-rescind-1776-commission-executive-order/index.html; see also Leanne Smith, "Hillsdale college grads say irony of president's statements calling minorities 'dark ones' was missed," *Mlive.com*, January 19, 2020, accessed on March 4, 2021, https://www.mlive.com/news/jackson/2013/08/hillsdale_college_grads_say_ir.html.

45. Ashton Pittman, "Trump Taps Ex-Gov. Bryant for '1776' Effort to Keep History Friendly to White 'Heroes,'" *Mississippi Free Press*, December 21, 2021, accessed on March 4, 2021, https://www.mississippifreepress.org/7725/trump-taps-ex-gov-bryant-for-1776-effort-to-keep-history-friendly-to-white-heroes/.

46. The 1776 Report, 20.

47. Ibid.

48. A PDF of the 1776 Report can be found here: https://trumpwhitehouse.archives.gov/wp-content/uploads/2021/01/The-Presidents-Advisory-1776-Commission-Final-Report.pdf.

Notes to Chapter 2

49. Alexander Solzhenitsyn, *Warning to the West* (New York, NY: Farrar, Status and Giroux, 1976), 33-34.

50. Quoted in David Solway, "Are the End Times Near?" (January 15, 2021), *American Thinker*, accessed on January 16, 2021, https://www.americanthinker.com/are_the_end_times_near_.html.

51. Letter from John Adams to James Warren, April 22, 1776, *Founders Online*, National Archives, https://founders.archives.gov/documents/Adams/06-04-02-0052. Original source: *The Adams Papers*, Papers of John Adams, vol. 4, *February–August 1776*, ed. Robert

J. Taylor (Cambridge, MA: Harvard University Press, 1979), 135–137.

52. Thomas Jefferson, "Letter to Roger Weightman," June 24, 1826, quoted in Levin, *Rediscovering Americanism*, 4–5.

53. The 1776 Report, https://trumpwhitehouse.archives.gov/wp-content/uploads/2021/01/The-Presidents-Advisory-1776-Commission-Final-Report.pdf, 3-4.

54. Ibid., 4.

55. "The Declaration of Independence and Natural Rights," *Constitutional Rights Foundation*, accessed on March 15, 2021, https://www.crf-usa.org/foundations-of-our-constitution/natural-rights.html.

56. Wilfred M. McClay, Land of Hope: *An Invitation to the Great American Story* (New York, NY: Encounter Books, 2019), 31.

57. Ben Shapiro, *How to Destroy America In Three Easy Steps* (New York, NY: Broadside Books, 2020), 16.

58. The 1776 Report, 2.

59. Ibid.

60. Ibid.

61. *The Declaration of Independence* (1776) in The U.S. Constitution and Other Writings (San Diego, CA: Canterbury Classics, 2017), 49.

62. Martin Luther King, Jr., "I Have a Dream," delivered August 28, 1963, *Yale Law School's Avalon Project*, accessed on March 15, 2021, https://avalon.law.yale.edu/20th_century/mlk01.asp.

63. Algernon Sidney, *Discourses Concerning Government*, quoted in *The U.S. Constitution: A Reader*, Hillsdale College Politics Faculty, eds. (Hillsdale, MI: Hillsdale College Press, 2018), 44.

64. John Locke, *The Second Treatise of Government* (1690), Thomas P. Peardon, ed. (Englewood Cliffs, NJ: Macmillan Publishing Co., 1952), 15.

65. Levin, *Rediscovering Americanism*, 6–7.

66. David Armitage, *The Declaration of Independence: A Global History* (Cambridge, MA: Harvard University Press, 2007), 3.

67. Ibid.

68. Robert R. Reilly, *America on Trial: A Defense of the Founding* (San Francisco, CA: Ignatius Press, 2020), 248.

69. The 1776 Report, 6.

70. Alexander Hamilton, quoted in *The U.S. Constitution: A Reader*, Hillsdale College Politics Faculty, eds. (Hillsdale, MI: Hillsdale College Press, 2018), 4.

71. Larry Arnn, quoted in *Ibid.*, 3.

72. Ibid.

73. The 1776 Report, 7.

74. Abraham Lincoln, "Fragment on the Constitution and the Union," quoted in *The U.S. Constitution: A Reader*, Hillsdale College Politics Faculty, eds. (Hillsdale, MI: Hillsdale College Press, 2018), 67.

75. Ibid., 68.

76. McClay, *Land of Hope*, 292.

77. Calvin Coolidge, quoted in *Ibid.*, 293.

78. Abraham Lincoln, "Speech at Lewistown, Illinois," August 17, 1858, quoted in Mark Levin, *Rediscovering Americanism: And the Tyranny of Progressivism* (New York, NY: Threshold Editions, 2017), 21.

79. Ibid.

Notes to Chapter 3

80. Fan Shen, *Gang of One: Memoirs of a Red Guard* (Lincoln, NE: University of Nebraska Press, 2004), 4.

81. Ibid., 12.

82. Ibid., 37.

83. Ibid., 14.

84. Jordan Peterson, *Maps of Meaning: The Architecture of Belief* (New York, NY: Routledge, 1999), 259.

85. Mao Tse-Deng, Speech at the Chinese Communist Party's National Conference on Propaganda Work (March 12, 1957), accessed January 7, 2021. https://www.marxists.org/reference/archive/mao/works/red-book/ch02.htm.

86. Wilfred M. McClay, *Land of Hope: An Invitation to the Great American Story* (New York, NY: Encounter Books, 2019), 3.

87. Terry Melanson, *Perfectibilists: The 18th Century Bavarian Order of the Illuminati* (Walterville, OR: Trine Day LLC, 2009), x.

88. Ibid., 18.

89. Immanuel Kant, quoted in Melanson, *Perfectibilists*, 8-9.

90. Ibid., 9

91. Ibid., 175.

92. Ibid., 58.

93. Ibid., 175.

94. Ibid., 27.

95. Ibid., 29.

96. Melanson, *Perfectibilists*, 60.

97. Ibid., 173.

98. See, for example, German Professor Reinhart Koselleck's 1959 work, *Kritik und Krise* (translated into English in 1988: *Critique and Crisis: Enlightenment and the Modern Society*), in which Koselleck asserts the Illuminati, along with Enlightenment philosophers and Freemasons were representative of a continuous ideological process which inevitably led to the cataclysm of the French Revolution. See also Richard van Dulmen's 1973 work, "Der Geheimbund Der Illuminaten" in *Zeitschrift fur Bayerische Landesgeschichte*, 36: 793-833. Also, his 1975 work, *Geheimbund der Illuminaten. Darstellung, Analyse, Dokumentation.* Also, James H. Billington, *Fire in the Minds of Men: Origins of the Revolutionary Faith* (Basic Books Inc., 1980), 6.

99. Joseph von Utzschneider, quoted in Melanson, *Perfectibilists*, 32.

100. Augustin Barruel, *Memoirs Illustrating the History of Jacobinism* [1798], quoted in Melanson, *Perfectibilists*, 97.

101. Melanson, *Perfectibilists*, 134-135.

102. Quoted in Melanson, *Perfectibilists*, 135.

103. Ibid.

104. Ibid., 136.

105. Ibid., 137.

106. Ibid., 138.

107. Ibid., 147.

108. Quoted in Melanson, *Perfectibilists*, 147.

109. Ibid.

110. Ibid., 9. The term "eugenics" was not coined until later in the nineteenth century.

111. Ron Gray, "Malthus was Wrong" (2001); quoted in Melanson, *Perfectibilists*, 10.

112. Phillip D. Collins, "The Ascendancy of the Scientific Dictatorship Part Two;" quoted in Ibid.

113. Ibid., 10.

114. See "Hegel's Dialectics" (2016), Stanford Encyclopedia of Philosophy. https://plato.stanford.edu/entries/hegel-dialectics/.

115. Antony C. Sutton, *America's Secret Establishment* (2002); quoted in Ibid., 11.

Notes to Chapter 4

116. Karl Marx, "Invocation of One in Despair," in *Early Works of Karl Marx: Book of Verse*, Marxist Internet Archive, accessed January 13, 2021, https://www.marxists.org/archive/marx/works/1837-pre/verse/verse11.htm.

117. Isaiah 14:12-15.

118. Karl Marx, "Letter from Marx to his father in Trier" (1837); quoted in *How the Specter of Communism is Ruling Our World*, 39.

119. Karl Marx, "The Pale Maiden," in *Early Works of Karl Marx: Book of Verse*, Marxist Internet Archive, accessed January 13, 2021, https://www.marxists.org/archive/marx/works/1837-pre/verse/verse11.htm.

120. Letter of Heinrich Marx, quoted in *How the Specter of Communism is Ruling Our World*, 39.

121. Karl Marx, "The Fiddler," in *Early Works of Karl Marx: Book of Verse*, Marxist Internet Archive, accessed January 13, 2021, https://www.marxists.org/archive/marx/works/1837-pre/verse/verse11.htm.

122. Richard Wurmbrand, *Marx & Satan* (Westchester, IL: Crossway Books, 1986), 37.

123. Karl Marx, *The Eighteenth Brumaire of Lois Bonaparte*, First issue of *Die* Revolution, 1852, accessed on January 13, 2021, https://marxists.architexturez.net/archive/marx/works/download/pdf/18th-Brumaire.pdf.

124. Karl Marx's letter to Ruge, September 1843, in *Letters from the Deutsche-Französische Jahrbücher*, accessed on January 13, 2021, https://www.marxists.org/archive/marx/works/1843/letters/43_09.htm.

125. Gareth Stedman Jones, Introduction to *Karl Marx and Friedrich Engels: The Communist Manifesto* (New York, NY: Penguin Classics, 2002), 94.

126. Ibid., 89.

127. Karl Marx, *Difference between the Democritean and the Epicurean Philosophy of Nature* (1841); quoted in Ibid.

128. Ibid., 95.

129. Marx and Engels, *Manifesto*, 218.

130. Vladimir Lenin, Preface to the Russian Translation of *Letters from J.F. Becker, J. Dietzgen, F. Engels, K. Marx, and Others to F.A. Sorge and Others*, in *Letters to Americans 1848-1895: A Selection*, Alexander Trachtenberg, ed. (New York, NY: International Publishers, 1969), 274.

131. Pinker, *Better Angels*, 343.

132. *How the Specter of Communism is Ruling our World*, The Epoch Times Editorial Board (New York, NY: The Epoch Times, 2020), 29.

133. Marx and Engels, *Manifesto*, 219.

134. Ibid., 222.

135. Ibid., 227.

136. Ibid.

137. Ibid., 229.

138. Ibid., 231.

139. Ibid.

140. Ibid.

141. Ibid., 232–233. In these passages, "bourgeoisie" and "proletariat" have been replaced with "oppressor class" and "oppressed class" respectively. This has been done to facilitate readability for those less familiar with the antiquated terms, and to make clear the ideology's fungibility depending on how a practitioner wants to define these classes (i.e. classes based on race rather than on economic stratification, such as Hitler did).

142. The term "cold civil war" has been used here and there online during the past several years to describe the increasing polarization and unrest in American domestic politics.

143. Marx and Engels, *Manifesto*, 231.

144. Ibid., 218.

145. Ibid., 234.

146. Ibid., 235.

147. Ibid.

148. Ibid., 237.

149. Friedrich Engels, "On Authority" (1872), Works of Friedrich Engels, accessed on January 16, 2021, https://www.marxists.org/archive/marx/works/1872/10/authority.htm.

150. Ibid.

151. Marx and Engels, *Manifesto*, 238-241.

152. Ibid., 238.

153. Ibid., 239.

154. Ibid., 240.

155. Ibid., 241.

156. Ibid., 249.

157. Ibid., 250.

158. Ibid., 258.

Notes to Chapter 5

159. D. Biderman, "Communist Attempts to Elicit False Confessions from Air Force Prisoners of War," September 1957, accessed on March 26, 2021; Biderman's PDF can be found here: https://apps.dtic.mil/dtic/tr/fulltext/u2/a484038.pdf.

160. Ibid.

161. Ibid.

162. "The Geneva Conventions of August 12, 1949," *International Committee of the Red Cross*, accessed on March 27, 2021; a text of the Geneva Conventions can be found here: https://www.icrc.org/en/doc/assets/files/publications/icrc-002-0173.pdf.

163. Ibid.

164. Carol Swain, "Carol Swain: 'Greatest threat' to society is 'diversity, equity, inclusion industry,'" *Be the People News*, February 19, 2021, accessed on March 27, 2021, http://bethepeoplenews.com/carol-swain-greatest-threat-to-society-is-diversity-equity-inclusion-industry/.

165. Ernest Hemmingway, *The Sun Also Rises*, quoted in Tim O'Reilly, "Gradually, the Suddenly," *Oreilly.com*, January 10, 2019, accessed on March 27, 2021, https://www.oreilly.com/radar/gradually-then-suddenly/.

166. Helen Pluckrose and James Lindsay, *Cynical Theories: How Activist Scholarship Made Everything about Race, Gender, and Identity—and Why This Harms Everybody* (Durham, NC: Pitchstone Publishing, 2020), 12.

167. Ibid., 15.

168. Ibid., 21.

169. Jordan Peterson, *12 Rules for Life: An Antidote to Chaos* (Toronto, Canada: Penguin Random House, 2018), 306.

170. Pluckrose and Lindsay, *Cynical Theories*, 13.

171. Ibid., 15.

172. Ibid., 18.

173. Ibid.

174. Ibid., 21.

175. Ibid., 23.

176. Peterson, *12 Rules for Life*, 310.

177. Pluckrose and Lindsay, *Cynical Theories*, 13–14.

178. Jonathan Butcher and Mike Gonzalez, "Critical Race Theory, the New Intolerance, and its Grip on America," The Heritage Foundation, Backgrounder, No. 3567, December 7, 2020, 4.

179. Martin Jay, *The Dialectical Imagination*, quoted in Butcher and Gonzalez, "Critical Race Theory," 4.

180. Nicola Pratt, "Bringing politics back in: examining the link between globalization and democratization," *Review of International Political Economy*, Vol. 11, No. 2 (May 2004), accessed on March 27, 2021, https://www.jstor.org/pss/4177500.

181. Butcher and Gonzalez, "Critical Race Theory," 5.

182. "Communist Party USA History and Geography," *Mapping American Social Movements*, James N. Gregory, dir. (University of Washington: accessed December 29, 2020).

183. Max Horkheimer and Theodor W. Adorno, *Dialectic of Enlightenment: Philosophical Fragments*, quoted in Butcher and Gonzalez, "Critical Race Theory," 5.

184. Butcher and Gonzalez, "Critical Race Theory," 5.

185. Manning Johnson, *Color, Communism, & Common Sense* (New York, NY: Alliance, Inc., 1958), 6-7.

186. Ibid., 7.

187. Ibid., 11.

188. Ibid., 12.

189. Ibid., 18.

190. Ibid.

191. Cornell Law School, "Critical Legal Theory," https://www.law.cornell.edu/wex/critical_legal_theory (accessed December 29, 2020).

192. Ibid.

193. Butcher and Gonzalez, "Critical Race Theory," 6.

194. Duncan Kennedy, excerpt of *Left Legalism/Left Critique*, quoted in Butcher and Gonzalez, "Critical Race Theory," 7.

195. Ibid.

196. Quoted in Butcher and Gonzalez, "Critical Race Theory," 7.

197. Ibid., 8.

198. David Horowitz, *Left Illusions: An Intellectual Odyssey* (Dallas, TX: Spence Publishing Company, 2003), 425.

199. Derrick Bell, "Who's Afraid of Critical Race Theory," quoted in Butcher and Gonzalez, "Critical Race Theory," 8.

200. Patricia Hill Collins and Sirma Bilge, *Intersectionality*, quoted in Butcher and Gonzalez, "Critical Race Theory," 9.

201. Helen Pluckrose and James Lindsay, *Cynical Theories*, quoted in Butcher and Gonzalez, "Critical Race Theory," 9.

202. Unpublished introduction to "Victoriosa Loquacitas," CWHN 10:243; *The Ancient State: The Rulers and the Ruled*, ed. Donald W. Parry and Stephen D. Ricks (Salt Lake City, UT: Deseret Book and F.A.R.M.S., 1991)

203. A PDF of the OMB memorandum can be found here: https://www.whitehouse.gov/wp-content/uploads/2020/09/M-20-34.pdf.

204. The entire eleven-page executive order can be found at https://www.whitehouse.gov/presidential-actions/executive-order-combating-race-sex-stereotyping/.

205. Ibid.

206. The memorandum can be found at https://www.whitehouse.gov/wp-content/uploads/2020/09/M-20-37.pdf.

207. Ijeoma Oluo, *So You Want to Talk About Race* (New York, NY: Seal Press, 2019), 252.

208. Ibid.

209. Ibid., xv, 1, 6, 12, 19, 28, 30, 41, 43, 251, and others.

210. Ibid., 19, 252.

211. Ibid., 232-233.

212. Ibid.

213. Elaine Donnelly, "The Military is Using Racist 'White Privilege' Materials, and the Next Funding Bill Would Make it Worse," accessed January 5, 2021. https://thefederalist.com/2020/09/29/the-u-s-military-uses-racist-white-privilege-materials-and-the-next-funding-bill-would-make-it-worse/?utm_campaign=ACTENGAGE.

214. Douglas Murray, *The Madness of Crowds: Gender, Race, and Identity* (Bedford Square, London: Bloomsbury Continuum, 2020), 52.

215. Ibid.

216. See a December 17, 2020 Secretary of Defense Memorandum here: https://media.defense.gov/2020/Dec/18/2002554854/-1/-1/0/ACTIONS-TO-IMPROVE-RACIAL-AND-ETHNIC-DIVERSITY-AND-IN-CLUSION-IN-THE-U.S.-MILITARY.PDF; see also the Special Operations Command Diversity and Inclusion Plan 2021 here: https://www.socom.mil/Documents/Diversity%20Mag%202021%20final.pdf.

217. Steven Pinker, *The Better Angels of Our Nature: Why Violence Has Declined* (New York, NY: Penguin Group, 2011), 479.

218. "Communism," The Martin Luther King Jr. Research and Education Institute, Stanford University, accessed on January 14, 2021, https://kinginstitute.stanford.edu/encyclopedia/communism.

219. Ibid.

220. Martin Luther King Jr., "Pilgrimage to Nonviolence," accessed on January 14, 2021, https://kinginstitute.stanford.edu/king-papers/documents/pilgrimage-nonviolence.

221. Yaron Steinbuch, "Black Lives Matter co-founder describes herself as 'trained Marxist,'" June 25, 2020, *New York Post*, accessed January 14, 2021, https://nypost.com/2020/06/25/blm-co-founder-describes-herself-as-trained-marxist/.

222. Ibid.

223. Ibid.

224. "Labor/Community Strategy Center," KeyWiki, accessed on January 14, 2021, https://keywiki.org/Labor/Community_Strategy_Center.

225. Black Lives Matter Global Network, "What We Believe," accessed July 2020, https://blacklivesmatter.com/.

226. Janaya Khan, "Janaya Khan on Black Lives Matter and The Art of Resistance," (February 15, 2017), *Flare*, accessed on January

16, 2021, https://www.flare.com/tv-movies/janaya-khan-black-lives-matter/.

227. F.A. Hayek, *The Road to Serfdom* (Chicago, IL: University of Chicago Press, 1944), 168.

228. Quoted in Rand Paul, *The Case Against Socialism* (New York, NY: Broadside Books, 2019), 245.

229. Julia Carrie Wong, "The Bay Area Roots of Black Lives Matter" (November 11, 2015), *SFWeekly*, accessed on January 17, 2021, https://www.sfweekly.com/news/the-bay-area-roots-of-black-lives-matter/.

230. Ibid.

231. Ibid.

232. Quoted in Ibid.

233. Ibid.

234. Ibid.

235. Ibid.

Notes to Chapter 6

236. Houston Keene, "Navy's 'extremism' training says it's OK to advocate for BLM at work but not politically partisan issues," *Fox News*, March 30, 2021, accessed on March 31, 2021, https://www.foxnews.com/politics/navy-extremism-training-black-lives-matter.

237. Jordan Peterson, *Maps of Meaning: The Architecture of Belief* (New York, NY: Routledge, 1999), 261.

238. Jim Garamone, "Austin Orders Military Stand Down to Address Challenge of Extremism in the Ranks," *DoD News*, February 3, 2021, accessed on February 4, 2021, https://www.defense.gov/Explore/News/Article/Article/2492530/austin-orders-military-stand-down-to-address-challenge-of-extremism-in-the-ranks/.

239. Phil Stewart and Idrees Ali, "Pentagon, Stumped by Extremism in Ranks, Orders Stand-down in Next 60 Days," *Reuters*, February 3, 2021, accessed on February 4, 2021, https://www.reuters.com/article/us-usa-biden-pentagon-extremism/pentagon-stumped-by-extremism-in-ranks-orders-stand-down-in-next-60-days-idUSKBN2A335W.

240. Ibid.

241. Ibid.

242. Garamone, "Austin Orders Military Stand Down."

243. Heather Mac Donald, *The Diversity Delusion: How Race and Gender Pandering Corrupt the University and Undermine Our Culture* (New York, NY: St. Martin's Griffin, 2018), 33.

244. Michael T. Rose, *A Prayer for Relief: The Constitutional Infirmities of the Military Academies' Conduct, Honor, and Ethics Systems* (New York University School of Law, 1973), accessed online on February 13, 2021, https://www.usafa.edu/app/uploads/A-Prayer-For-Relief-Final-5.16.11.pdf.

245. "Policy Proposal: An Anti-Racist West Point" (June 25, 2020) can be read online here: https://s3.amazonaws.com/static.militarytimes.com/assets/pdfs/1594132558.pdf.

246. Helen Pluckrose and James Lindsay, "How to be Not-Racist," *New* Discourses, October 23, 2020, accessed on February 8, 2021, https://newdiscourses.com/2020/10/how-to-be-not-racist/#post-3679-Anti-Racism.

247. Ibid.

248. David Horowitz, *Left Illusions: An Intellectual Odyssey* (Dallas, TX: Spence Publishing, 2003), 75.

249. Ibid., 76.

250. Ibid.

251. Ibid., 376.

252. Ibid., 377.

253. Ibid.

254. Ibid.

255. The full text of the 1962 Port Huron Statement can be found here: http://www2.iath.virginia.edu/sixties/HTML_docs/Resources/Primary/Manifestos/SDS_Port_Huron.html.

256. Brian Albrecht, "Strongsville woman graduates at top of class at U.S. Military Academy," *Cleveland.com*, June 10, 2018 (updated January 30, 2019), accessed on February 9, 2021, https://www.cleveland.com/metro/2018/06/strongsville_woman_graduates_a.html.

257. James Lindsay, "OnlySubs: Call Them 'Neoracists,'" *New* Discourses, January 29, 2021, accessed on February 8, 2021, https://newdiscourses.com/2021/01/onlysubs-call-them-neoracists/.

258. Mary Esch, "Army Splits with West Point Tweeter of 'Communism Will Win,'" *Military News*, June 19, 2018, accessed on Feb-

ruary 9, 2021, https://www.military.com/daily-news/2018/06/19/army-splits-west-point-tweeter-communism-will-win.html.

259. Brent Briggeman, "Air Force football takes firm social stance with video in support of Black Lives Matter," *Gazette*, July 7, 2020, accessed on February 13, 2021, https://gazette.com/sports/air-force-football-takes-firm-social-stance-with-video-in-support-of-black-lives-matter/article_559d1a60-c08b-11ea-a070-f367d3b16347.html.

260. *Black Lives Matter and the Hatch Act*, dated July 14, 2020, U.S. Office of Special Counsel, https://www.usgs.gov/media/files/office-special-counsel-advisory-black-lives-matter-and-hatch.

261. United States District Court for the District of Maryland, *Standage v. Braithwaite*, Civil Action No. ELH-20-2830 (December 22, 2020), file:///C:/Users/Matt/Downloads/Standage%20v.%20Braithwaite.pdf., 5.

262. Ibid.

263. Ibid., 6.

264. Ibid., 4.

265. Ibid.

266. Ibid.

267. United States District Court for the District of Maryland, *Standage v. Braithwaite*, Civil Action No. 1:20-cv-02830, Document 98-2 (Filed February 15, 2021).

268. Ibid.

269. United States District Court for the District of Maryland, *Standage v. Harker*, Civil Action No. 1:20-cv-02830, Document 98 (Filed February 15, 2021).

270. "Midshipman Chase Standage should be separated from the Naval Academy for racist comments," *Change.org*, created by Cleo Fontaine, accessed on February 15, 2021, https://www.change.org/p/superintendent-shawn-buck-midshipman-chase-standage-should-be-separated-from-the-naval-academy/sign.

271. United States District Court for the District of Maryland, *Standage v. Harker*, Civil Action No. 1:20-cv-02830, Document 98-4 (Filed as Supplemental Reply Exhibit B on February 15, 2021).

272. Ibid.

273. The best analysis of Antifa's training and radical plans to date is journalist Andy Ngo's new work *Unmasked: Inside Antifa's Radical Plan to Destroy Democracy* (New York, NY: Center Street, 2021).

274. "John Schofield: the Navy and Naval Academy should take notes; Spicer and Standage must go along with Trump," *Capital Gazette*, January 10, 2021, accessed on February 15, 2021, https://www.capitalgazette.com/opinion/columns/ac-ce-column-john-schofield-2021113-20210110-7x3ernv5jrhxfltct5qjk3pe5a-story.html.

275. Ibid.

276. United States District Court for the District of Maryland, *Standage v. Harker*, Civil Action No. 1:20-cv-02830, Document 91 (Filed on February 4, 2021).

277. Ibid.

278. Ibid., 4.

279. United States District Court for the District of Maryland, *Standage v. Harker*, Civil Action No. 1:20-cv-02830, Document 98 (Filed on February 19, 2021).

280. Ibid.

281. Ibid.

282. Elizabeth McLaughlin, "Gen. Charles Brown confirmed as next Air Force chief of staff, becoming first black military service chief in American history," *ABC News*, June 9, 2020, accessed on February 12, 2021, https://abcnews.go.com/Politics/gen-charles-brown-confirmed-air-force-chief-staff/story?id=71152066&fbclid=IwAR04fFPCsVMkuESzSh7z1OMEYoVruAoVqvFWj9uImSZ2LemBoWZUkMbH5BE.

283. The IRDR can be found here: https://www.af.mil/Portals/1/documents/ig/IRDR.pdf.

284. Jack Phillips, "Black Lives Matter, Antifa March through DC, Chant 'Burn it Down,'" February 7, 2021, *The Epoch Times*, accessed February 7, 2021, https://www.theepochtimes.com/black-lives-matter-antifa-march-through-dc-chant-burn-it-down_3688149.html?utm_source=news&utm_medium=email&utm_campaign=breaking-2021-02-07-2.

Notes to Chapter 7

285. F.A. Hayek, *The Road to Serfdom* (Chicago, IL: University of Chicago Press, 1994), 169.

286. Fan Shen, *Gang of One*, 12.

287. Ibid.

288. Ibid.

289. Ibid., 13.

290. Ibid., 13-14.

291. Ibid., 14-15.

292. Ibid.

293. Ibid.

294. Ibid., 15-16.

295. Ibid.

296. Ibid., 16-17.

297. Steven Pinker, *The Better Angels of Our Nature: Why Violence Has Declined* (New York, NY: Penguin Group, 2011), 321.

298. Ibid.

299. Ibid.

300. Ibid.

301. In his book *How to Destroy America in Three Easy Steps* (2020), Ben Shapiro explains that there are three elements that have enabled America to stay a country: American philosophy, American culture, and American History. To destroy these is to destroy America.

302. Thucydides, quoted in Stathis N. Kalyvas, *The Logic of Violence in Civil War* (New York, NY: Cambridge University Press, 2006), 78.

303. Kalyvas, *The Logic of Violence*, 64.

304. Ibid.

305. Ibid.

306. Ibid., 81.

307. Ibid.

308. Ibid.

309. Ibid.

310. Ibid.

311. Ibid., 82.

312. Ibid.

313. Ibid.

314. Alexander Solzhenitsyn, "Repentance and Self-Limitation in the Life of Nations," in *From Under the Rubble* (Boston, MA: Little, Brown and Company, 1974), 109.

315. Ibid.

316. Air Force leaders, for example, are now asserting that too many of the service's pilots are white, a problem the service is seeking to remedy. "Colorado Springs Gazette: Don't dismiss skills to pursue military diversity," *Colorado politics*, March 30, 2021, accessed on April 1, 2021, https://www.coloradopolitics.com/opinion/editorialroundup/colorado-springs-gazette-dont-dis-miss-skills-to-pursue-military-diversity/article_eced7af2-91cf-11eb-bbc9-57df087c7274.html.

ABOUT THE AUTHOR

Matthew Lohmeier is a 2006 graduate of the United States Air Force Academy. He began his active-duty military career as a pilot, flying over 1,200 hours in the T-38 as an instructor pilot followed by the F-15C. After flying, he cross-trained into space operations and gained expertise in space-based missile warning. In October 2020, he transferred into the United States Space Force. He has two master's degrees—a master in military operational art and science, and a master of philosophy in military strategy. Currently, he is a lieutenant colonel in command of a space-based missile warning squadron in Colorado, where he lives with his wife and children.

CPSIA information can be obtained
at www.ICGtesting.com
Printed in the USA
LVHW110334220521
688188LV00018B/683/J